REVEREND DEVIL

REVEREND DEVIL

Master Criminal of the Old South

by

ROSS PHARES

PELICAN PUBLISHING COMPANY

GRETNA 1974

Published by Pelican Publishing Company, Inc.
630 Burmaster Street, Gretna, Louisiana 70053

To
MRS. CAMMIE GARRETT HENRY
of Melrose Plantation

CONTENTS

REVEREND DEVIL

CHAPTER I

A WAYSIDE TAVERN

IT was the first hour after dark. A woman and a boy
sat in a small, dimly lighted room. Adjoining was a
larger room, the small lobby of a wayside tavern, and from
it came the incoherent murmur of dull voices. Otherwise
all was quiet. A gesture from the woman, and the boy
drew his chair nearer, and the two sat very close together.
The boy leaned nearer that he might not miss a word.
The woman was the boy's mother, and she was about to
send him on an errand. Unlike most boys, this one was
thrilled, and he listened to his mother with a cunning
smile on his face. The woman mumbled a few sharp sen-
tences into the boy's ear. He understood. He admired
his mother; and he was happy.

The mother had other children, but this one was her
favorite. He always listened carefully, he was clever, and
his mother had learned that he was dependable.

The woman eased away, quietly, bluntly. She was
a busy woman with duties to attend. She was manager
of the inn, which served also as a home.

The boy did not go to his task at once. It was necessary for him to wait. Already he had learned the great
lesson of patience. The errand would be done when the
time came. While the mother went about the business of
placing the guests in their rooms, the boy sat quietly in

the outer room, like a well trained child. Travelers commented that he was a bright boy.

That night a peddler was robbed at the inn. The boy
had performed his assigned task. With a bunch of trunk
keys, which he had made a hobby of collecting, he had entered the peddler's room, unlocked one of his trunks and
taken a bolt of fine linen and several other items. The
trunk was re-locked; and the next morning the traveler,
not suspecting any foul play, paid for his lodging and rode
off down the trail as a regular satisfied customer.

It was years later before this act became public. The
boy had grown into a handsome man. His very name had
become a word of horror; and he had broken all records
as an outlaw.

It was not an important haul, but John A. Murrell
felt proud of his clever bravery. "I thought that was not
a bad figure I had made," he said of it. Perhaps it was
not for a boy of ten.

John A. Murrell was born about the year 1800. The
exact place of his birth is not known. But at an early
age he was living in Williamson County in or near the little village of Bethesda, about twenty-five miles south of
Nashville.

Bethesda, Tennessee, was a quaint and serene little
community surrounded and half hidden by the foot-hills
of the Cumberlands. It was a beautiful dreamy region of
green hills and swift, rock-bedded streams. It was an
ideal place for hunting and fishing and swimming. But
if John A. Murrell was charmed by this picturesque setting
with its natural advantages he never spoke of it. From
his earliest days, he was more interested in "speculations."

John watched the traffic go by over the Natchez
Trace. This fascinating pageant that constantly paraded

by inspired him strangely. And he took an absorbing interest in the travelers who put up at the tavern. These guests brought breath-taking stories of spectacular robberies and fabulous loots, of smart tricks of the outlaws, and the lurking dangers of the wilderness road. And the dark headed boy would sit motionless and tense listening, with a glow in his wide eyes. He dreamed of the day when he too would ride along the mysterious trace seeking adventure and fortune.

The Murrells were a strange family. William (?) Murrell, the father of John A., was a minister who preached salvation and the way of righteousness to the world at large, and let his family run wild at home. Tennessee historians described him simply as a "Methodist preacher having a good moral character." John A. said of him: "My father was an honest man I expect, and tried to raise me honest, but I think none the less of him for that." At home the Reverend William Murrell was "a good man, but not energetic." Doubtless he had some influence in the pulpit, but at home such was not the case. During the working days of the week the minister took a very insignificant role. William Murrell was a henpecked husband who sat back meekly and let the "old lady" run things. He did not manage the affairs of the tavern; he did not—doubtless could not—manage his family. "He was not energetic."

The mother was the head of the family. She managed the tavern as well as the affairs of the family; and it was she who guided the boyish footsteps of John and started him on the road to everlasting fame. "My mother was one of the true grit; she learned me and all her children to steal as soon as we could walk. . . . . Whatever we stole she hid for us, and dared my father to touch us for it.

She made us hate the proud ones that had niggers most—after those who had more than we."

The mother was of the mountain stock, whose ancestors had supposedly been of that group of assigned servants who, in early imigration days had been committed and sold for terms of years varying with their offenses, the men of whom "affected a sullen familiarity with their neighbors of higher degree, and swore great oaths over the fact that there was no approach to sociability between their wives and daughters and those whom they called disdainfully, as their remote ancestors had called in good faith, 'the quality.' " But John was proud of his mother. "My mother was of the true grit . . . she came of the mountain stock."

It is probable that the father was of the same stock. But whatever it was John never bragged about it.

It is not known for sure how many children grew up in the wayside inn. There was a daughter, Elizabeth, and a younger son named William. If there were others they escaped record.*

As a lad John was always looking about for some smart scheme. When he was sixteen he learned a new trick by accident. One day he walked into the store of a neighboring merchant, and through a mistake the storekeeper spoke very politely, calling him by the name of a young man who had a rich father, and invited him to trade with him. The boy, always alert, thanked him and requested him to put down a bolt of superfine cloth. He

---

* There was a James Murrell who got into trouble with John and William during their early days. The trouble in which James was involved was minor, and after the paying of a slight fine he passed out of the picture. He may have been a brother, a cousin, or neither.

took an expensive suit and had it charged to the rich man's son.

It is not clear just how John spent the next four years of his life after swindling the storekeeper. Some of his time was passed selling a few of his neighbors' horses, without the owners' knowledge; and it seems probable that he was dabbling in highway robbery.

He was gaining a considerable reputation. Suspicious people began watching him too closely for his comfort and convenience. John decided that the place was too small for him anyway; so he "concluded to go off and do my speculation where I was not known, and go on a larger scale."

From the tavern home John headed north for Nashville.

CHAPTER II

A BAD START

IN the second decade of the nineteenth century Nashville was still a backwoods town of approximately five thousand inhabitants. On top of the bluff overlooking the steamboat landing was the public square, in which stood the courthouse, surrounded by a hitchrail. From this square the town spread out in all directions.

Compared to other towns of the American frontier, Nashville was quiet as well as strict. But Nashville was not asleep, nor were the inhabitants a colony of sissies. Next door to the inn was a vacant lot reserved for cock fights. The Clover Bottom race track was one of the best known in the West. Certainly the town was not without entertainment and excitement. Fast horses and charming ladies were the topics of the day. Men killed for the sake of their honor and the name of their women.

But a peculiar form of rigid frontier justice existed in the Nashville vicinity. Crime barely showed its head there. Men liked to boast that Nashville was clean. The mild recreation of playing billiards was very popular, but a law was passed branding the game a "wicked" luxury, and a tax of one thousand dollars a table was imposed for

this vile pleasure. For years the stocks, whipping post
and branding iron for minor offenders were well used instruments. Horse stealing carried the penalty of death
without benefit of clergy.

The officials who made and upheld the laws were
products of the rough, severe frontier. They were men
who wore buckskin breeches, used profanity profusely,
fought duels, drank hard liquor, went to cock fights on
Sundays, and bet liberally on horse races. But they maintained a rigid honor peculiar to the frontier. Typical examples of such men were Andrew Jackson, Thomas H.
Benton, and Sam Houston. Offenders both feared and respected such characters. There was no compromise with
men of this type. Nashville early became the training
ground for statesmen, and the dread of outlaws.

But Murrell came prancing into the mountain town
on his fine horse with little thought of the real temper of
the place. He made a flashing, gay debut. His suit was
of the finest cloth and showed immaculate tailoring. His
hat was of the latest style. He carried his head high; his
pride was evident. He had money, and he had already
acquired the habit of spending it freely. It gave him
pleasure to have people think him wealthy.

Soon Murrell was strutting along the streets there,
looking for "friends in this business." There was an air
about the young fellow that attracted attention and impressed people. He had a knack for winning friends. His
address was pleasant and gentlemanlike, his manner cordial and frank. There was something about the well-
poised young man that made people want to obey him.

Somewhere on the streets of Nashville Murrell met a
man by the name of Daniel Crenshaw, a high-spirited,
heavy-set man with a round face, a jolly eye, and a bad

reputation. The two had a long talk.

Crenshaw was a man of adventurous spirit. He talked of big and bold things. The two made congenial company. But it was clear that Nashville was not the place for them.

A few days later Murrell and Crenshaw were riding over the wilderness road toward Georgia with a drove of stolen horses.

Along the edge of the Cumberlands a young South Carolinian, Woods by name, fell into their company. Woods found the two talkative "horse-dealers" delightful company. Crenshaw showed a polite interest in the young man's business. Woods was pleased. He told his interested companions everything. He had been to Tennessee to buy a drove of hogs, but he had found pork so much higher than he expected that he had made no purchase. He was on his way home without the pork and with the price of the hogs still in his pocket.

Crenshaw winked at Murrell. The men understood each other. Near the top of one of the mountain ridges "Crenshaw asked me for my whip, which had a pound of lead in the butt; I handed it to him." The rest was simple enough. The entertaining Carolinian, still commenting upon the price of hogs in his best style, paid no attention to the fatal preparations going on about him. Murrell with sudden enthusiasm pointed out across the valley at some imaginary sight. Woods lengthened in his stirrups and stretched his neck for a better view. But the view never appeared. Crenshaw, at the moment close in on the other side, came down with a crushing blow upon the man's head with the butt of the whip. He slumped from his saddle, stunned, but not dead.

"We lit from our horses and fingered his pockets; we got twelve hundred and sixty-two dollars. Crenshaw

said he knew a place to hide him, and gathered him under
the arms, and I by his feet, and conveyed him to a deep
crevice in the brow of the precipice, and tumbled him into
it." And so the body, yet alive, went crashing into the
tree tops below. "That ought to break him up some,"
said Crenshaw. They did not have time to do a neater
job of it. The road was well-used. Travelers might be
appearing any time.

They flung the victim's saddle and equipment over
the precipice after him; his horse was run into the drove.
And again the men went riding on down the trace.

But for some reason they changed their course. They
headed for Alabama.

As the men jogged on over the stony mountain road,
Crenshaw fell to telling more of himself. And his young
companion listened eagerly. What mettle this man Crenshaw had!

Crenshaw told many stirring stories of his adventures
and travels. According to Crenshaw's own statements he
had mixed in everything from highway robbery to murder.
He had, in his earlier days, made a voyage out from Bara-
taria with Lafitte and his pirates, and he had been ship-
wrecked off the Isle of Pines. They were all lengthy and
romantic tales that made the long journey entertaining.

In Alabama the drove of horses was sold for "a good
price." And then the frolic began. "We were the highest
larks you ever saw. We commenced sporting and gambling, and lost every cent of our money."

But Murrell was not a man to go without money for
long at a time. An empty purse usually stimulated some
recuperative idea. Upon entering a small town in Alabama, Murrell sensed a situation that proved a lasting inspiration. He and Crenshaw immediately decided that it

was entirely unnecessary that they remain penniless any longer.

They found the town in confusion. Armed guards were patrolling the streets, shops were closed, an air of apprehension hung over the place, business was at a standstill. A rumor had been spread about that the slaves were planning an uprising. People had been living in dread for some time that the negroes might rebel. Many of the inhabitants were of the impression that the Spaniards wished to incite such a rebellion because Alabama had been added to the American Union in 1819 in spite of many protests from Spain. The long territorial dispute between Spain and the United States left hatred behind between the two races. It seemed for a while that there would be serious trouble.

In most towns the slaves outnumbered the whites. That Spain might incite a rebellion of the slaves was terrible to think of. At the slightest hint of such a disaster whole counties would spring to arms. In this town the slaves had been warned, under penalty of death, not to leave their cabins after nightfall. Women did not venture out of doors without armed escorts. Children were watched closely, even indoors.

In the general confusion no one paid much attention to the two strangers who rode carelessly into the excited town on two fine horses. Everybody was watching the negroes, and planning to suppress possible rebellions. It was a rich opportunity for the two rovers, and they were quick to take advantage of it. The two men stayed several days in the town, looking the situation over well. They made plans and awaited their opportunity. On their last night they took what goods they needed from the stock at a local store, waylaid a few late strollers and relieved their pockets of all valuables. Next day they left as unobserved as they came. It was the negroes who were blamed for the crimes.

The clever gentlemen rode on toward Mississippi. It was a good haul they had made, and Crenshaw was anxious to get to the city to spend his easy money. He spoke of the fun he had enjoyed in New Orleans and Memphis.

But Murrell seldom spoke now. He was thinking. What he had seen at the Alabama town had made a profound impression upon him. What tremendous effects even the rumor of a negro rebellion could cause! Suppose, then, a real uprising could be brought about — a well planned, skilfully maneuvered rebellion on a large scale! With everybody afraid of the slaves, looting would be easy. The idea of a negro uprising was a mere germ of a scheme, but he could not forget it.

At the time, Murrell's experiences were limited; he did not know how such a scheme could be accomplished. But he believed in it, with vague understanding. It was a hazy, indefinite thing, a sort of wild fantasy with no more shape than a nightmare. But the very bigness, the drama of such action fired his imagination. He did not even discuss it with Crenshaw. He just rode silently on, his fist clenched about the saddle horn with a savage tension, his jaw locked a little firmer, a strange distant look in his dark eyes. He would wait.

After a wandering trip over Alabama and Mississippi the Tennesseeians landed back in their native state. It had been an eventful journey, this first extended adventure of John A. Murrell. And it was a bold partner who had accompanied the young outlaw.

In Nashville the two outlaws parted company. And several years passed before the two worked together again. But in the meantime, both received some bitter experiences.

In 1826 Crenshaw's name became prominent in the court records. In January of that year he was charged with forging a note on the Bank of Tennessee for two hundred dollars; the following month he stole a horse worth seventy-five dollars from Kessiah Wooldridge; and in April he made away with another horse worth one hundred and ten dollars belonging to a lawyer by the name of R. C. Foster. He was charged with all three offences in separate indictments. In April he was brought to trial in Franklin for the stealing of R. C. Foster's horse.

This was the last of the three offences with which the defendant was charged, the Wooldridge and Bank of Tennessee offences having occurred before. Crenshaw was tried according to the procedure of the day, found guilty of horse-stealing, and sentenced. The sentence was light according to the day and the offence, but it was a gruesome affair, at that.

The defendant was sentenced to six months imprisonment. But, as was the custom of the day in dealing with horse thieves, he was first led out to the "block" on the public square to be branded on the thumb with the letters "H. T." (horse thief). Here, in the presence of the judge and sheriff and an informal gallery of gaping spectators, the grim procedure took place. Tradition has it that Crenshaw was defiant, that as soon as the branding was finished, and while his hand was still smoking from the effect of the hot iron, he bit the letters from his thumb with a savage wrench of his hand and spat the mangled bit of flesh at an attendant.

A queer statute and the brilliant pleading of a young ambitious lawyer by the name of John Bell saved Crenshaw from the penalty of the other two crimes. Doubtless Bell had little faith in Crenshaw's innocence, but he was eager to make a name for himself and he believed that the laws with which the case dealt — passed in the days of Henry VIII and Elizabeth — were out of date. It was the wish of the bar that he should make a test case of the trial.

As soon as Crenshaw had been branded and sent to jail to be whipped, pilloried, and imprisoned, Bell asked permission of the court to withdraw the pleas of "Not Guilty" in the two remaining cases. The request was granted, and he then filled in each case a plea of "Benefit of Clergy" in which he claimed that Crenshaw, having been punished in part for one offence and having been duly branded, could, under the law of Benefit of Clergy, demand the right to be exempted from punishment for all offences, short of capital, that may have been previously committed. The plea was overruled, and thereupon Bell appealed the case to "the Superior Court."

There Crenshaw was acquitted. And immediately afterwards the antiquated "Benefit of Clergy" law was repealed.

It was a noted trial, the decision was precedential, and the participants historical figures. The opinion was rendered by Judge John Catron, who later was for many years a justice of the United States Supreme Court. Bell was elected to Congress the next year; and he in turn became Speaker of the House, Secretary of War, and candidate for president.

After Crenshaw served his short term in jail for the first charge he became a free man again. He dashed back into the obscurity of the wilderness, and his trail was not picked up again until he joined Murrell several years later.

The bad influence of Crenshaw upon Murrell has been stressed, and in some instances over-rated. Doubtless because of the fact that Crenshaw was older and a hardened criminal when the two began "running together,"

Crenshaw has been credited with being the leader, and the man chiefly responsible for leading Murrell astray. But if Crenshaw was ever the leader he never held the position long. Murrell was a man born to lead; and hardened and notorious as Crenshaw may have been, he was soon overshadowed by the younger man; and his importance sank into insignificance compared with that of the ambitious Murrell.

When Murrell returned home from his tour with Crenshaw he was carrying his head a little higher; he felt proud of himself. He believed that he was a man of the world. "I had become a considerable libertine, and when I returned home I spent a few months rioting in all the luxuries of forbidden pleasures with the girls of my acquaintance."

It was quite a figure that the dashing, romantic Murrell made, entertaining the mountain girls. Six feet or more in height, he was an imposing sort of fellow with his dark wide eyes that seemed both friendly and dangerous. A handsome, smartly-dressed dandy he was, with a swagger and a gay spirit that the country girls could not resist. The older folks commented more about his "important" bearing, his commanding gestures, his grace of manner. Nature had done much for Murrell.

All might have been well, but the young bandit ran out of cash. The home girls got all of his money; and he was not yet through having fun. So to recoup his fortune he set out to steal a bunch of horses.

But he failed to do it. Instead, he got caught in the act, and was pushed into a court room at the point of a shotgun.

Murrell fought the charge. The case was delayed, shifted from court to court, and finally brought to Davidson County on a change of venue. Apparently the defendant's reputation was such in Williamson County — where the crime had been committed — that prejudice was too strong to guarantee an unbiased trial.

It appears that at an earlier trial he had been sentenced to three years imprisonment. But his final trial brought him a shorter term. It was the sentence of the court that "John A. Murrell shall receive on his bare back at the public whipping post in Davidson County thirty lashes, set in the pillory two hours on Monday, two hours on Thursday, and two hours on Wednesday, next, that he be branded on the left thumb with the letters H. T. (horse thief) in the presence of the court; that he be imprisoned twelve months from this day and be rendered infamous."

It was on Saturday, a day when the country folk had flocked into town, that John A. Murrell was publicly whipped and branded. A crowd was loafing at John Wright's store, across from the court house, when someone suddenly exclaimed: "There goes Jo Horton with John Murrell taking him to the court house to be branded." The word spread out. Soon people came beating it to the court house from all directions to see the spectacle.

Inside the courtroom, the handsomely dressed Murrell was led to the prisoner's box, a square, partly enclosed seat near the railing that surrounded the judge's stand. He was directed to lay his hand on the railing. He extended it as casually as if for a handclasp. Sheriff Horton then took from his pocket a piece of new hemp rope and bound the hand securely to the railing.

But there was a delay. The iron was not hot. And so Murrell sat there, silently, facing the wide-eyed herd that had swarmed in to see the show.

Presently a big negro came in bringing a tinner's stove. He placed it on the floor in front of Murrell. Sheriff Horton delayed a moment. He turned the iron over, and held it in the clear flame for a few seconds. It was red hot. Then quickly, as if for fear the instrument might cool, he plunged it onto Murrell's motionless hand. The frying skin crackled, and the smoke rose two or three feet before the branding iron was lifted. Then the sheriff unbound the hand; and Murrell, who up to the time had not moved, produced a white handkerchief and wiped it several times. It was said that Murrell perhaps showed less emotion than anyone in the courtroom.

When it was all over, Murrell was led back to the jail to wait for the execution of his other penalties.

Later he was led out to the public whipping post. He did not have his well-groomed appearance now, for he had been stripped to the waist. But he walked erect, and with a natural dignified grace. There was a firm, chiseled look upon the man's face. He showed neither fear nor contempt. He said nothing. His reserve was almost freakish.

But after ten blows from the heavy whip Murrell asked for time to rest. Each lash had left an open, bleeding gash. The man had almost lost his breath. Then he braced himself again, and the torturing ordeal went on while the crowd of curious spectators looked on.

Several times before the thirty lashes were completed Murrell had to ask for time to rest. The requests were granted, but the process went on until the last stinging blow was laid on the prisoner's bare back.

When the ordeal was finished Murrell was motionless. He looked limp and pale. It seemed that the man had fainted. He had to be told that it was all over. But in a moment he was himself again. He walked away as calmly as he came. There was something uncanny about the man's composure.

It was perhaps, in part, because of his lack of any show of pain that the lashes had been so heavy. It was said that Murrell barely twitched a muscle. He never groaned, and he never asked for mercy, just for time to catch his breath. The man's stubborness was only equaled by his efficacious reserve.

It may have been that Murrell had never planned murder as part of his career, and that Crenshaw was the one responsible for the terrible disposure of the young South Carolinian. But from that horrible day on, Murrell was an embittered man, with a passion for revenge.

Murrell was carried back to jail to serve his sentence.

Inside the stone walls Murrell made a queer prisoner. He kept a stack of old books stored away in his cell; and during the long months of his solitary term he would be seen hour after hour pouring over them, a strange searching gleam in his hard-set eyes. And a strange library these volumes made for a convicted horse thief—a Bible

and a group of law books. But they absorbed him, and
hour on end he sat over them, bent and motionless, as if
poisoned into a death stiffness. No one knew the man's
thoughts as he sat there in the dim light reading, thinking,
planning, scheming for the future. He seldom spoke.

Until the last day of his term he continued his study
of criminal law and fundamental theology. "During my
confinement I read the scriptures, and became a good judge
of theology. I had not neglected the criminal laws for
many years before that time. When they turned me loose
I was prepared for anything." And it seemed that he
was!

CHAPTER III

THE WILDERNESS

WHEN the doors of the prison were finally drawn open and Murrell stepped out, a free man again, he found his brother William waiting for him.

The two lost no time. John was restless, and he wanted to talk. They headed toward the Choctaw Nation on two fine, freshly-stolen horses.

As the brothers rode over the wilderness road that led to the Choctaw Nation John told of his plans and his hatred. Horse stealing was all right, but he had better and more profitable plans. And these so-called smart judges and lawyers would not touch him. He knew more than they did now. He had not spent his lonely months studying for nothing. His voice trembled with passion as he told William what they would do in the Choctaw Nation. He had the eagerness and suppressed rage of a wild caged animal. He was ready to strike back!

Negro stealing! A shrewd man who knew the law could steal negroes and get by with it. John delighted in telling how the law could be evaded. "It is the law that settles all these matters," he said. "Let a man learn the use of the law, and nothing can touch him." He told the younger brother how he figured to beat the law in running off slaves. To be caught stealing a negro would mean a serious sentence. But there was no need of one getting in bad over a negro slave, John explained. He was too shrewd for that. He would persuade the negroes to run off from their masters of their own free will. Then he would hide them and wait until the owner advertised a reward.

According to the laws of that day, such an advertisement amounted to the same as a power of attorney for a finder to take a slave and hold it for the owner. The law was good enough for honest men. But if a man wished to take the advertised slave for his own use instead of carrying him to the lawful owner, that was not stealing, and the only way the owner could get the slave was through a process of law.

There were many advantages to negro stealing. A negro might be stolen over and over again. And a slave might help to steal himself. If a slave became too well advertised he might easily be permanently disposed of. John had studied that feature of the work also.

In the wilderness frontier who was there to stop a shrewd man who knew the law?

The frontier was still an untamed country, too young for much organization. But all types of people had seen opportunities there; and they had marched boldly into it with little fear of its dangers or hardships. First home-seeking pioneers had pushed into the forest, cleared a fertile spot in some creek bottom, and built a log cabin; and after them, all sorts and classes of men came: farm hands, mechanics from the city, carpenters, traders, pack-peddlers, soldiers of fortune seeking employment and adventure in the new country. The supreme attraction was the "Valley," that great wild space that bordered the Mississippi from the mouth of the Ohio to the Gulf. It was called a land of new opportunities and new hopes; and to it had tramped the disappointed, the embittered and the suppressed, some seeking solitude, and others seeking escape. In the procession came speculators, gamblers, desperadoes, and escaped convicts; and most notable of all the horse thief, the counterfeiter and the robber. Every man to his own trade. Here men carried on about as they pleased, and the wilderness held its secrets.

The thinly settled country rendered arrest and conviction difficult, if not impossible. The numerous water courses — the rivers, the winding bayous and creeks, the lakes — covered on all sides with swamps and canebrakes, made escape easy. Once the outlaw dashed into the thick undergrowth, pursuit was almost impossible. Nature had done much for the outlaw.

When Murrell first traveled the narrow trails that led over the rolling hills of west Tennessee and through the canebrakes and bottoms on to the great Mississippi, the solitary gloom of the deep woods had gripped him. He too had spun his dream of fortune and adventure.

John Murrell knew the histories of the earlier outlaws, daring men who had appeared singly and in all forms of organization along the Mississippi. "These men had the nerve for anything, and nobody stopped them," he reminded William, as they rode through the shadows. And to inspire the younger brother he told amazing stories of the most famous of them, tales that had been handed down with more bragging and exaggerations than truth, no doubt; but these romantic accounts formed a sort of legendary *Who's Who* of the infamous, and all the outlaws learned them as if a part of their education.

Among the earliest robbers were Mike Fink, Sam

Crity and their associates, and outlaws of Cave-in-Rock on the Ohio — no one knew how many. Before the days of the steamboats, there was a class known as "boat-wreckers," the most noted of which was a gang commanded by "Colonel Plug," whose headquarters were near the mouth of Cash Creek, a short distance above Cairo. Wherever there was traffic on the Mississippi there had been pirates and terrifying crimes that could not be forgotten. There were times when the marauders all but controlled the Mississippi. The Spanish government early took organized means to suppress them, but without success. When the United States came into possession of both banks of the river, the pirates were stronger than ever. Then the new government took up the fight against them. But it seemed that nothing could be done about the condition. These facts amused John Murrell. Two governments had tried, and still the outlaws were in power!

But it was the present and the future that John wanted to talk of most. Fresh out of his cramped prison cell, he wanted to speculate upon bold plans and weave vast thoughts that knew no bounds. On either side of the horsemen, tall trees and thick undergrowth hedged the narrow road and made it a mere half-hidden winding streak through the virgin forest. It was a stimulating country to John Murrell. Dark, mysterious, unlimited, he felt that here almost anything might be done, and he told William so. He felt free and at home once more.

William listened with confused interest. He was not so sure of himself as John. But he too had had his disappointments and misfortunes.

Apparently William had, at one time, entertained some idea of leading a straight life. He began a professional career as a school teacher. It was at Salem

Church in the Yellow Creek bottoms that the young peda-
gogue started out. The outlook seemed bright enough. But
a discipline problem clipped the teaching career of young
professor Murrell distressingly short. It was in the days
when the rod was considered a most important, as well as
necessary, part of the school equipment. One day he
whipped a young girl by the name of Maddin, and the report was that he whipped her "unmercifully." Whether
that was true or not, the mother of the child was wrought
up over the affair to the extent that she paid the schoolmaster a visit; and she brought along an "apron full" of
stones. And so terrible was her volley of rocks that professor Murrell was forced to flee. This may have been a
turning point in his life. Anyway, he never returned to his
task. The patrons of Salem Church School were soon hunting for a new schoolmaster, and ex-professor Murrell began hunting his neighbors' horses.

The end of the journey proved a disappointment. Prospects were not as good in the Choctaw Nation as the Murrell brothers had expected.

But John would not consent to leave empty handed.
Somewhere near the Nation they found an old negro and
his wife and three sons who were very anxious to become
free. John decided right then to show William the ways
of his new trade.

John told the black family that if they would work
for him and his brother for a year they could go free after
that. He told them their new home would be Texas, a delightful land where negroes were free and happy and had
plenty of everything.

There was an air about Murrell that made people,
especially negroes, want to trust him. And so the negroes,
thinking this smooth talking, sympathetic gentleman the

greatest man on earth, gleefully wrapped up a few of their belongings and deserted their cabin.

But Murrell never intended carrying the black family to Texas, or freeing them either. He was not interested in Texas, or the Choctaw Nation, or Tennessee now. Shortly out of prison, he wanted to taste the pleasures of life. So he turned his face toward New Orleans, that wicked, glamorous city at the mouth of the mighty Mississippi. Stories were ever coming up the great river of the reckless pleasures to be found in the crescent city. It was a city to dream about, and every young man of the Valley longed to behold its wonders. The black family went along. There must be some business on the way, or there would be no pleasures at the end. It was a long journey. But Murrell would smile as he told William what they would do in New Orleans.

CHAPTER IV

CITY OF SIN

The trip to New Orleans was a difficult and trying one. The brothers got lost in the Mississippi swamps. The ground became so boggy for their horses that they had to turn them loose and wade in on foot. But even then they could not find the river.

Days later, when they finally sighted the river, they were no better off. There was no boat, their food was gone, they were exhausted, and still lost. William grumbled and cursed their luck. But John was calm. He had plans, and plans take time. William marveled at this hardy brother's patience and the manner in which he took hardships.

John left the party and eased into a thicket that grew on a mound of high ground near the river. A few shots were heard. And when he emerged again he carried an armload of wild game. Before a blazing fire the men cooked and warmed themselves. They ate and felt stronger.

Then the party splashed into the slushy swamp again, but they were in better spirits now. The negro family, plodding along behind, whispered among themselves of the good times they would have down in Texas when they would be free and their troubles all over. The white brothers also spoke of good times — fast amusement they

would find in New Orleans. Finally they stumbled upon
an Indian trail which wound its way through the bottom
to a bayou. Following the course of the bayou they came
to the river again, and there they had the good fortune of
finding a large canoe locked to the bank. The boat was
immediately broken loose; and soon the party was floating
with the river current toward New Orleans.

The trip down the river might have been pleasant and
agreeable enough had not the old negro become suspicious
that the white men were going to sell him and his family.
He heard no more talk of Texas, and he became more uneasy as time passed, and grew contrary. Murrell would
have none of that. He was an executive who carried on
his business according to plan; he never tolerated com-
plaint, and most of all he took no unnecessary chances.
"We saw that it would not do to have him (the elder negro)
with us; so we landed one day by the side of an island,
and I requested him to go with me round the point of the
island to hunt a good place to catch some fish. After we
were hidden from our company I shot him through the
head and ripped open his belly, filled the hollow with sand
and tumbled him into the river. I returned to my company,
and told them that the negro had fallen into the river and
that he never came up after he went under."

Fifty miles above New Orleans the party landed and
went into the country. The old negro's suspicion proved
a prophecy. The remaining negroes were sold to a Frenchman for nineteen hundred dollars. That was enough to
last a while!

They dressed themselves "like young lords," and hurried on to start their spreeing in the tempting city.

New Orleans was a place to attract adventurous men
of Murrell's mold — desperate, reckless characters, who

lived by chance and held life cheap. In this strange city almost anything might happen. Fortunes might be earned or taken at the point of the gun or the turn of a card. Life was swift, carefree; pleasures were cheap. People asked few questions. Life was lived for the present. Such a spot had a natural appeal for the daring, pleasure-loving Murrell.

From a few straggling wood structures in the great bend of the Mississippi, New Orleans had grown steadily into a large, picturesque, cosmopolitan city. The town had first been French, then Spanish; and when the Americans came it was neither French nor Spanish but Creole, a blending of both. New Orleans was different from other American cities. It was a bright, glamorous place, a city of amusement and excitement, and of luxury and extravagance. A dream city, indeed! If New Orleans grew less mysterious with the years, it certainly grew more colorful. Men of all breeds gathered here as the city enlarged, and for all purposes.

Up from the river, on beyond Gallatin Street, was the beautiful New Orleans, a city of swaying palm trees, picturesque old dwellings with spacious courtyards, and city squares. In the coffee shops varied groups enjoyed conversations as varied as their complections: Farmers from the large plantations in the parishes back of the city; Creole gentlemen, talking of the theatre and opera; blonde Germans from the coast; young dandies with money to buy the city's pleasures; Spaniards from Texas and Spain's western dominions; aristocratic Americans seeking business and pleasure at the same time; and among all, a sprinkling of tourists from perhaps a dozen foreign countries. Travelers came from every where. For here were the operas, theatre, the circus, bull fights, balls, music, and games of chance that stirred the senses. New Orleans was

famous for rich and cultured men and women, characters
who lived for excitement — lived for the present and made
the most of it. On Royal Street gentlemen and aristocratic
Americans cast their cards against the professional gamblers of the river; it went on day and night.

Down along the levee was a different society, coarse,
dirty, vulgar. But it was as much New Orleans as that
around Jackson Square. Tied up to the wharf were boats
of every description, fleets of flatboats and barges from
up the river, trading brigs from across the sea, Indian
canoes here and there which had floated in from the
bayous, and a few crude steamboats. Below the levee in
the shanties dwelt the strange crews that manned the
vessels tied up on the water front. In the late evening as
the sun began to sink behind the city, the shipmen swarmed
along the levee awaiting the pleasures of the night. And
a motley herd they made. There were seamen from a
dozen nations, red-shirted Kentucky flatboatmen, mariners
from the Orient, steamboat captains and negro porters.
And here travelers met a kindred society, reckless, bold
and daring as they — swaggering bullies, professional
gamblers and sharpers, fugitives from justice, blanketed
Indians, garlanded Creoles, trappers in buckskin, laughing
mulatto girls, barefoot slaves. It was a hard-living, fear-
less, reckless tribe that swarmed here in the late evening.

Along the river front Murrell made his debut. He
strutted along the rough streets in his well-cut broadcloth
suit and his high topped silk hat. He was a man to command attention. Here were men of his mold, and women
who had cast their lot with the worst. The section was a
hive of energy, a gathering place of roughs and scalawags,
gamblers, gunmen and thugs who swarmed in for the pickings, land buccaneers and pirates from the Gulf, men of
spent lives and forlorn hopes, men without country, reli-

gion, or honor. No wonder New Orleans was called the "City of Sin!"

On the levee this motley crew lingered to spend their hard-earned dollars, to fight, to get gloriously drunk and sing their dirty songs, and squall out their vulgar yells and curses. These reckless rovers wooed adventure like a mistress; and many, intoxicated with the lust of gain or the passion for pleasure, robbed right and left, killed their victims and sent corpses splashing into the muddy river, only to plunge back into the wilderness that gave them birth.

The most reckless spot in the city was Gallatin Street.* Murrell visited there often. He braved its dangers and partook of its wild pleasures. The gay bandit loved to tell of pleasures and excitement he found there. He never came to New Orleans that he did not visit Gallatin Street.

It was the first thoroughfare parallel with the river, a very short street; narrow, with high buildings and over-hanging balconies. It was a place where cheap women and dirty sailors met for the companionship of a night. Gambling and drinking went on constantly. The air reeked with the smell of cheap liquor and the stench of unventilated rooms that seldom saw light. Dangers lurked in every corner of its dark alleys.

But Gallatin Street, with all its exciting pleasures, could not hold the Tennessee bandit for long. In New Orleans Murrell saw crimes committed on an extensive scale, with little interference. He sensed the possibilities of vast exploits here. It put his growing ambition on edge. Soon he was mixing pleasure and business to advantage.

*Gallatin Street ceased to exist in 1937. Its old buildings were torn down to make room for an addition to the famous French market. Today the locality is known as "Market Place."

"I mixed with the loose characters of the Swamp (that region of shanties and shacks in the mud flats across the river) every night." Murrell made many interesting and valuable friends there. Some he met quite by accident:

One night as he was returning to his boarding place he was stopped by two armed men who demanded his money. Murrell handed them his pocket-book, and while doing so remarked that he was very happy to meet them as they were all of the same profession. One of them observed: "Damned if I rob a brother chip." The robber explained that they had had their eyes on him for several days, and had judged by his fine clothes and glittering jewelry that he was some wealthy dandy with a surplus of cash, and had determined to rid him of the trouble of some of it. "If you are a robber, here is your pocket-book, and you must go with us tonight, and we will give you an introduction to several fine fellows of the block." The men set out to find the gang. But suddenly one of the bandits stopped bluntly as if he had overlooked something important. He called for Murrell's attention: "Do you understand this motion?" he questioned, giving a peculiar flirt of the wrist. Murrell answered the secret outlaw sign, and without further ado they hastened on for a few drinks to celebrate new friendships.

"We went to old Mother Surgick's, and had a real frolic with her girls. That night was the commencement of my greatness in what the world calls villainy. The two fellows who robbed me were named Haines and Phelps; they made me known to all the speculators that visited New Orleans, and gave me the name of every fellow who would speculate that lived on the Mississippi River, and many of its tributary streams, from New Orleans up to all the large western cities."

Murrell learned fast of the wicked vices of the "City

of Sin." He made many new acquaintances who were to
prove of real value. And he knew how to use "friends"
to advantage. How many men the outlaw robbed while
on this visit to the city can never be known.

He considered the robbing of a certain Kentuckian
one night unusually amusing. It was a rare case of robbery without murder. Excuse for this irregularity was
apparent:

Murrell had become acquainted with a Kentuckian,
who boarded at the same tavern where he was staying.
The young Kentuckian had floated down the river on a
raft with the product of several seasons to sell at the market city. It was quite natural that he should have lots of
money. Murrell thought so; and he was a very good judge
of such matters. "I felt an inclination to count it (his
money) for him before I left the city." So Murrell made
his notions known to Phelps and a few other of his new
comrades. A plan was concocted.

That night Murrell and the jolly Kentuckian had a
few drinks together and went off to the Swamp on a spree.
They had become very intimate, and the Kentuckian
thought his gallant, polished friend one of the best fellows
in the world. The Kentuckian was very fond of wine;
and Murrell was generous that night. They were in for
a real frolic. They drank and told funny stories and "cut
a few shines with the girls," until much of the night had
passed. Then they started for the tavern. Murrell knew
what was coming, but the Kentuckian, happy with generous wine, never dreamed that their night of joy could
be spoiled so rudely. About half way to the tavern, at a
spot previously agreed upon, the frolicing pair was met by
a band of robbers. Both men were cleaned. The Kentuckian was so furious that he cursed the whole city and
wished that it would be deluged in a flood of water as soon

as he left the place. But little good did his raving do.
Murrell spent a few soft words to console the heart-broken
boatman who had lost his entire fortune. It might happen
anywhere. Murrell cursed a bit too, just to be congenial.
It was too bad! They both would have to start all over
again.

Next day the Kentuckian left the city on foot to wind
his long route back up the Valley to his native state, broke,
disgusted, and damning the evil city. The same morning
Murrell went to his friends and got his share of the spoil
money, and his purse of which he had been relieved. Seven
hundred and five dollars of the Kentuckian were divided
among thirteen of the gang.

After a few weeks the Murrell brothers left New Orleans in grander style than they had entered. John had
learned to love the exciting city.

In the years to come John visited New Orleans frequently, to carouse, to rob and kill, to exchange counterfeit
for good American dollars, to sell stolen negroes.

There is another account of a visit to New Orleans
with stolen slaves. It was different from the earlier journey. This time the traveler was a bolder outlaw, more sure
of himself, with more knowledge of the law and less fear
of it, with a system of villainy gaining perfection. The
distinguished negro-stealer on this trip was traveling in
the best of style, dressed like a lord, conversing with the
best society on board the river ship, giving the general impression that he was a man of wealth and culture and dis-
tinction. No one on board looked finer. He had his
negro with him, but that only added to his prestige.

The younger brother, then living in Tipton County,
Tennessee, had decoyed a negro boy from his master and

appointed a place for the boy to meet him. A friend was sent for the boy, to convey him to the Mississippi River, where a skiff received the two and conducted them to Natchez. Here the run-away slave was lodged secretly in the care of a second friend.

At Natchez John took charge of the boy, who to all appearance, had been purchased as a body-servant, and boarded a steamboat for New Orleans. All might have been merry sailing had there not been a passenger on board who knew Murrell well. The man went to the captain and told him that the negro which Murrell had was stolen property and that Murrell was a noted negro thief. He recommended to the captain that he take the black boy into custody and carry him back up the river. The owner's advertisement would likely be found when the boat returned.

The captain, perhaps in the hope of getting a reward and the services of the negro for some time—or maybe it was through his sense of duty and justice—took the advice. The boy was taken into custody and was not allowed to see Murrell. The slave told nothing. In fact, he thought Murrell was his legal owner.

There was little that could be done. The situation would have been embarrassing for any other person. But Murrell had been in close places before. He knew how to handle such matters. He called the captain an old villain and a rascal who was trying to take advantage of him and take his body-servant. Passengers on board believed Murrell. Who could doubt a man with such genteel manners! Patiently he waited until the boat reached New Orleans, and as the boat was landing he ducked off without being seen.

Down in the Swamp the outlaw joined his friends, and he had many of them now. He told them how he had been

mistreated while coming down the river. It was an out-
rage! So Murrell went to the mayor of the city, and
after telling his story, secured a process against the captain for unlawfully detaining his property from his possession. A guard was sent to take the captain, which
was done just as he was preparing to start his boat. He
and the negro were both taken before the Mayor.

In the presence of the mayor Murrell charged the captain with having detained his property from his possession
by violence and force of arms. He produced a bill of sale
for the negro, purporting to have been given in Tipton
County, State of Tennessee, and brought in a witness (one
of his comrades from the Swamp), who swore that he was
present when the negro was purchased, and saw him delivered to the plaintiff.

"What evidence do you have to support your claim?"
the mayor asked the captain.

The captain, somewhat baffled by this strange turn
of events, replied that he was told that the man was a
negro thief.

The mayor frowned.

"And what are you going to do with the slave?" the
officer continued.

"I was going to keep him, sir, . . . keep him safe."

That was enough. The gavel sounded. It was time
for justice to be meted out. For a man to be deprived of
his property was bad enough, but for a gentleman to be
called a negro thief in the presence of his associates and
be humiliated was a slam at decent society.

It was the captain who was "kept safe" for a while.

The negro was delivered to the plaintiff, and the captain was given a heavy fine and imprisoned.

When Murrell had not returned to the ship for his
negro, the captain had naturally thought that the thief had

been fortunate enough to get a chance to run, and was glad to cover himself. Murrell had waited until the captain was ready to leave before he effected his arrest. And so it was that the shipman had no chance to prepare any defence. "New Orleans is a minute place," Murrell remarked.

The obliging fellow who had informed the captain was Murrell's next concern. Murrell was not a man to let such matters slip by unnoticed and without proper attention. First, such characters were a great hindrance to his traffic, and, in the second place, the observing meddler might go back home and tell something. "And so for the captain's pretty friend who knew so much, he soon had a nurse that tended him day and night, until he found his way to the bottom of the river."

A few days after he recovered his Tennessee negro, Murrell sold him for eight hundred dollars; and in a few days he stole him again.

Business attended to, Murrell plunged again into the shadows of Gallatin Street and the cheap pleasure houses of the Swamp to drink, to frolic with the girls, to plot with his comrades, to curse society.

From Basil Hall

NEW ORLEANS RIVER FRONT—ABOUT 1830

CHAPTER V

ON THE SOUTHERN CIRCUIT

WHEN John A. Murrell appeared in the Valley again a
miraculous change had taken place with the man.
He was now riding along the winding roads that joined
the Southern plantations, astride the best horse that good
judgment and clever thievery could provide. He was wear-
ing a long coat and a long face. An air of pious dignity
hung about the erect, well-dressed man in the saddle.
Ex-convict Murrell had become a wealthy Methodist minister, and he had set out to preach salvation to the South.

Explanations have been attempted for this strange
turn of life. Doubtless it was Murrell's home life, more
than anything else, that brought his morbid attitude toward religion. Murrell remembered much of the habits
and manners of the Methodist preacher from his father.
Certainly he knew enough to put the act on in grand style.
Murrell had watched the religious activities of his meek,
hen-pecked father, for whom he had no respect, with both
amusement and contempt. But from him he learned much

of the ways of the minister. Apparently the Reverend William Murrell was a conscientious, religious man who meant well, and who had a sincere zeal to spread the gospel of his belief. And in spite of the fun poked at him at home, he went among the simple mountain folk of his faith preaching to little congregations here and there in his own humble way. But all the glory of the Sunday meetings disappeared when Reverend Murrell came home. Here he was just another lazy, shiftless husband. His religious efforts made both him and his religion appear ridiculous in the eyes of his family. Doubtless John first read his father's Bible through curiosity, and then for the purpose of fitting himself to poke fun at religion. The father could exert no good influence upon his son. It was the mother whom John admired. There was a woman with grit! She earned the living, she cursed the aristocrats who had more, she cursed religion, and she taught the children a trade.

As a child John A. had been amused at the blind confidence a minister of the gospel could inspire, even a sorry minister like his father. Murrell had no respect for his father. From the time he began to learn the first meaning of things, John looked upon the ecclesiastical efforts of his submissive father as a great joke. But the alert boy had seen the effect that a man could have who could read the Bible and shout at the people from over it. Murrell possibly did not understand this strange pulpit influence. But he adopted the device of the clergy, much perhaps in the same manner as a magician who does not understand his own trick, but knows well its effect.

For a long time Murrell thought over the preaching idea. But he could make nothing definite of it. He, by nature, was much too restless to settle down as the pastor of some church. And, though he might have had some fun with such an arrangement, there could never have been a great deal of excitement and no "speculation" for long at a time. It was left to a man named Carter to suggest a plan whereby the idea could be developed into an extensive system for crime. Carter told Murrell that there was no necessity for a man settling down in a definite locality in order to preach. A man of Murrell's calibre and temperament should be a traveling evangelist.

Murrell met Carter while the two were carousing in the red-light district of Natchez. Murrell was a bitter man, burning with a desire to outdo all the other outlaws in crime, to avenge society. Carter was clever and well known. "He was highly respected by all who knew him, and well calculated to please." Murrell could use such a man.

Down under the Hill, Carter was known as a rip-roaring, handsome fellow who partook freely of the sensuous pleasures that the section afforded. But on the road this charming libertine was a changed man. He traveled disguised as a Methodist minister. Murrell admired this queer gospel shouter. "He was as slick on the tongue as goose grease," Murrell related admiringly.

At Walton's Tavern-bar Murrell and Carter sat long over their glasses, talking in low tones that were almost whispers. Nobody noticed. Such was common in the dens along the water front, that section of Natchez known as Natchez-under-the-Hill. It was here that the outlaw world met and planned and plotted.

For a long time Murrell had been turning a big plan over and over in his mind. During his silent prison term he had set for hours studying, tense and motionless, as if paralized by the magnitude of his own idea. Later as he rode along the wooded trails he thought of it, aboard the steamboats his mind was constantly molding this wicked child of his warped ambition. Yet he never told anyone what it was. But he was always hinting something that sounded big to the outlaws. Why shouldn't the outlaws organize! Hadn't society done so! The wilderness was changing. It was being cleared away and roads and fields were appearing, travel was swifter, news spread quicker, and the communities were keeping in closer touch with one another. Whereas the outlaw used to run loose in the dense forests and swamps without fear of detection, the lone bandit was now in danger. He might be tracked, hedged in. Descriptions of men could spread faster now. The real change had not come, but Murrell saw that it was near. How long the solitary fugitive might run amuck and rob and kill without any great danger, he could not say. But sooner or later it must end—if men under the crust of society did not organize as their hated superiors in the comfortable cities on the hills had done. They must strike back. Murrell was too shrewd to be caught again! And he wanted to do something bigger than steal and rob.

As Murrell sat there in Walton's tavern, leaning heavily over the rough table, slowly sipping his bitters, he told Carter what he and Crenshaw had seen in Alabama—a town panicky with fear of a negro rebellion. It was such men as Carter whom Murrell wished to meet, men who had ideas, smart men who could help him plan and organize.

Soon the two clever gentlemen emerged from the red-light district of Natchez-under-the-Hill and began a series of revival meetings in the Valley, exhorting sinful congregations along the Mississippi to follow the straight and narrow path.

It was an interesting trip, indeed, that these two gay young hypocrites made over the South, shouting sermons, singing psalms, praying long prayers for lost souls, pass-

ing out counterfeit currency, running off negroes, unload-
ing stolen slaves. If it was Carter who suggested the idea
of an evangelical tour, it was Murrell who perfected its
use as an instrument in crime. How long the two men
worked together is not known. But before long the Reverend John A. Murrell so over-shadowed his brother in
the service that Carter was heard of no more.

The time was ripe for such adventurers as Murrell.
And Murrell was always quick to sense the advantage of
a situation. The West at this period was a rich field for
the smart man. It was a day of innumerable quacks and
charlatans of all varieties. The mountebanks were constantly pouring into the country with their miracle rem-
edies, Seneca oil for rheumatism, skunk oil for colds, herb
tonics for all ailments. Any clever trick was capital.
People would collect from miles around at the summons of
a sign board announcing the prospective arrival of a Hindu
magician. The people were humbugged over and over.
They liked it. Long coats and high-top hats were symbols
of superiority, honor, intelligence. The fast tempo of the
West gave the settlers little time to investigate a stranger
further than his garments. Most anyone could qualify
for the bar. Courts were a mass of confusion. Wildcat
bankers flourished, and their worthless paper money flood-
ed the Valley. Swindlers built imaginary towns in the
West, and with maps and pictures thereof sold town lots
to Eastern "suckers."
The arrival of an itinerant preacher in those times
was an event to bring settlers from miles around. When
such an event was to happen, tidings of it were spread far
and wide, and on the appointed day there assembled a
company drawn from all the country around. The religious temperament of the people was typical of the time

and place—feverish, emotional, fickle. The Westerner
looked with awe upon all things religious. The minister
was the most respected of people. Most persons looked
upon him as a superior being whose character was never
to be questioned. He was the direct representative of the
Deity; his words were the guided creations of the Holy
Ghost.

The sermons of these backwoods preachers were full
of hell-fire and brimstone. They preached a strict religion and they shook their congregations with a fear of
blazes and damnation. One observant writer of the period
wrote: "They (the ministers) could describe the Kingdom
of Heaven more minutely than most men of the present
day could describe their wives' bedrooms; they could give
a full bill of fare of all the pleasures indulged in there,
also a programme necessary to be followed in order to obtain admittance; but when they came to Pluto's region,
they became omniscient—could dwell for hours on that
horrible lake of fire and brimstone in which all sinners,
particularly those who lived within five miles of their min-
istration and failed to attend, were doomed to wiggle
through eternity."*

Another writer told of these old-time meetings.
Though perhaps a bit bias, the account shows keen observation:

"They (the camp meetings) were numbered among
the errors of the past. They constituted the largest gathering that met in the early days. Races, fairs and monkey-
shows were comparatively small concerns, as these only
drew the wicked, and were suspended on Sundays, while
camp-meetings drew all sorts, particularly the women,
who, of course, drew the men, especially when they found

* Davis, **History of the City of Memphis**, 219.

themselves in a triumphant majority, as was the case in
this country at this time. The very homeliest woman in
the country could get as many beaux as she wanted, while
the beauties wielded a sway that was truly distressing.
These meetings always continued for a week, commencing
on Thursday and ending on the following Wednesday.
Sunday was the big day of the occasion, when all the big
guns were brought out and the grand rally for mourners
came off. The town and country sent its thousands to
swell the crowd, which found ample provisions for its com-
forts, including a dozen or more booths in different directions, a quarter of a mile or less from the main shed, com-
posed of brushes cut and piled up, behind which was concealed a barrel of whiskey. The proprietors were supplied
with an ample number of junk bottles and runners to attend customers at the shed, where the bottles would be
passed around, sometimes within a few yards of the speaker's stand, until their contents were exhausted, when they
would be dispatched back with the necessary fee for re-
filling; and its effects may be readily imagined. There
may be some who think that a camp meeting is no place
for love-making; if so, they are much mistaken. When
the mind becomes bewildered and confused, the moral re-
straints give way, and the passions are quickened and less
controllable. For a mile or more around a camp ground
the woods seem to be alive with people; every tree or bush
had its group or couple, while hundreds of others in pairs
were seen prowling around in search of some cozy spot."*

Curious performances attended these revival meetings.
Services have been described as a "frothing frenzy." Men
and women went into emotional fits. They were high-
tension, noisy, often terrifying affairs. Strong men shout-

---

* Keating, **History of the City of Memphis and Shelby County.**

ed and rolled and tumbled in the aisles; the women clapped their hands loud in a primitive rhythm, uttered unnatural screams in high pitched voices, their muscles jerking. These nervous attacks often went on for hours. Another contemporary wrote:

"The bodily agitations and exercises attending the excitement in the beginning of this century were various, and called by various names, as the falling exercises, the barking exercises, the laughing and singing exercises, and so on. The falling exercise was very common among all classes, the saints and sinners of every age and grade, from the philosopher to the clown. The subject of this exercise would generally, with a piercing scream, fall like a log on the floor or earth, and appear as dead. . . .

"The jerks cannot be so easily described. Sometimes the subject of the jerks would be affected in some one member of the body, and sometimes in the whole system. When the head alone was affected, it would be jerked backwards and forwards, or from side to side, so quickly that the features of the face could not be distinguished. When the whole system was affected, I have seen the person stand in one place and jerk backward and forward in quick succession, the head nearly touching the ground behind and before. Though so awful to behold, I do not remember that any one of the thousands that I have seen thus affected ever sustained any injury in body.

"The dancing exercises generally began with the jerks, and was peculiar to professors of religion. . . . The barking exercise, as opposers contemptuously called it, was nothing but the jerks. A person affected with the jerks, especially in the head, would often make a grunt or bark, from the suddenness of the jerk. . . . The laughing exercise was frequent—confined solely to the religious. The running exercise was nothing more than that persons feeling something of those bodily agitations, through fear, attempted to run away and thus escape them; but it commonly happened that they ran not far before they fell, where they became so agitated they could not proceed any further. . . . The singing exercise is more unaccountable than anything else I ever saw. The subject, in a very happy frame of mind, would sing most melodiously, not from the mouth, or nose, but entirely in the breast. . . . It was most heavenly.

"These revival meetings led directly to the campmeeting. Everyone wished to attend them, but the country was sparsely settled and those at a distance were precluded from them unless they came and wished to camp in the vicinity of the place where the services were held."

Such meetings were described as "a storm that purifies the atmosphere." Some of them, however, were quieter and more peaceful:

"At night the grove was illuminated with lighted candles, lamps and torches. The stillness of the night, the serenity of the heavens, the vast crowd of attentive worshippers wrapped in a deep solemnity which covered every countenance, the pointed and earnest manner in which the preachers, in different portions of the vast concourse, exhorted the people to repentance, faith and prayer, denouncing the terrors of the law upon the intemperate, produced the most awful, solemn sensations in the minds of all."*

Murrell had looked on at these performances as a boy. As he grew older he studied the naive, passionate temperament of the people of his day; his insight into human nature was one of his most valuable accomplishments. He soon learned how easy it was to hoodwink a

---

* Moore and Foster, **Tennessee the Volunteer State, 1769 - 1923,** 332.

man once his religious fever had been aroused. His attack
on society was no less vengeful than other outlaws of his
day, but he was subtle. He found that in the frenzy of
a heated revival most anything could happen.

Murrell quickly learned the tricks of the trade. He
never carried off property himself. He kept with him a
corps of assistants to attend to the details of the work.
There were generally three of these brothers, two of whom
would travel along incognito and attend all revivals, while
the third would appear as a close associate and confidential friend of the evangelist. He was the personal worker
of the troupe. Brother Murrell's stewards understood
him well. A mere gesture from the divine and they were
about their duties. While the congregation would be as-
sembling he made it a point to mingle with the good people, accompanied by his personal worker, shaking hands
with as many as he could; and in so doing he would indicate his choice of horse-flesh to his good steward in somewhat the following manner:

"Glad to see you out tonight, Brother Brown," he
would say over a firm hand clasp. "That's a fine horse
you have." Or "Glad to meet you, Brother Smith. I see
you are a good judge of horses. I'd like to own an animal
like that." In this manner he would greet the members
of his congregation, and thus select perhaps a dozen of
their best horses. And then while he exhorted the sinners,
and pointed out to them the way of the light, beseeching
the blessings of the Deity upon his flock, his two anony-
mous assistants, having been advised by the personal worker, would be saving the best horses from the hitch rack
for the parson. No one would ever have suspected the
tall, sanctimonious man in the long coat who held on so
tenderly to his black-back book.

On one occasion he was entertained in the home of

a good Methodist by the name of Nobs, who, at the time, resided on the Elk River in middle Tennessee. Nobs had heard his guest preach some time before in the neighborhood, and was much impressed with him as a preacher. He was flattered that the distinguished minister had accepted his invitation. Murrell gave his residence as South Alabama, and while in Brother Nobs' home he spoke a great deal of his farm and negroes. The evangelist lamented that he had difficulty in getting an overseer who would do his duty, and not abuse his slaves. Such cruel persons, these overseers! Brother Nobs was touched. Conversation was interrupted by the call to supper. As was quite the custom, the visiting parson was lengthy in his supplications at the table. He raised his hands in the most solemn manner "as though he was just going to open the windows of heaven, and select its richest blessings for Brother Nobs, his wife, and latest posterity."

Nobs was a religious man, and before retiring he handed the family Bible to his reverend guest, to lead the family prayer service. In the "use of the book . . . . he was eloquent." The walls resounded long with the beseeching tones of the kneeling man as he lead the family circle in solemn prayer. The same service was rendered the next morning.

When about to depart, he wanted to pay Brother Nobs. But Brother Nobs was almost hurt to think that his guest would suppose he would charge a minister of the gospel for a night's lodging. The evangelist pushed his hands into his pockets. He was out of change. Would Brother Nobs be so kind as to give him change for a twenty-dollar bill? He disliked to offer a bill of that size to be changed at lodging places. "For," as he explained, "the world will say he is a preacher and does not like to pay for staying at night at a tavern—see, he has presented a twenty-dollar bill to be changed." His pride would not stand it. "This is the way of the world, and I hope God, in his mercies, will enable me to live in such a manner as never to dishonor the cause of the gospel, or degrade the ministry."

Brother Nobs was anxious to render the preacher, whom he thought to be a rich man, a service. He ran to his wife and got the trunk key, took out the purse, and counted out seventeen dollars and fifty cents, when, alas, his change ran out. The good Methodist host was distressed. "Stay a little," he said, "and I will run over to Brother Parker's and borrow the balance."

"Do, if you please," responded the obliged minister, "and I will stay with Sister Nobs until you return."

It was not long before Brother Nobs returned, half out of breath. He counted out the correct change with pride. Brother Murrell was grateful. He lingered a few moments longer engaging in courteous conversation. Then a fine-looking animal in Brother Nobs' barnyard engaged the departing man's attention.

"Well, Brother Nobs, you have a fine young jack. Did you raise him?"

"He was foaled mine, and I have raised him."

"Will you trade him, Brother Nobs?"

"I have raised him for that purpose, but I cannot get the worth of him in this country. I have been offered more than one hundred and fifty dollars for him; and he is worth two hundred and fifty."

"Yes, Brother Nobs, he is cheap at that price; and if I had the money with me I would rid you of any further trouble with him."

"Well, Brother, you can take him," the proud owner responded. "You say you will be at our camp meeting. Bring me the money then. That is as soon as I will need it."

"Well, Brother Nobs, I will take him. I want him
for my mares. I am a domestic fellow; I raise my own
mules for my farm."

The trade was completed; the jack was caught and
haltered, then all the family gathered around to receive
the good man's parting blessing.

"Brother Nobs, May the Lord bless you, and save you
in Heaven; farewell, Sister Nobs, may the grace of our
Lord and Saviour Jesus Christ rest and remain upon you;
farewell, and may the Lord bless your little children."

Thus departed the evangelist from the home of Mr.
Nobs and the little community on Elk River. And that
was the last Brother Nobs ever saw of his smart guest
who left him a twenty-dollar counterfeit bill and led off
his fine jack.

Murrell did not go to South Alabama where he had
told of his plantation and beloved slaves. Instead, he
headed for the western district of Tennessee. The preacher was delayed by his slow-traveling jack. But two days
later he sold the animal for four hundred dollars, and was
again on his voyage of soul-saving.

In New Orleans the tired evangelist tarried for a few
days rest and relaxation on Gallatin Street, and incidentally to dispose of a few stolen slaves.

Refreshed after a brief vacation from the pulpit, he
started North again with one slave, a favorite body-servant.

Somewhere in one of the parishes north of New Orleans he preached for a community of Methodists, where
resided a certain Mr. Higginbotham. It was with pride
that Mr. Higginbotham invited the visiting preacher into
his home for a few days, and showed him the best hospitality that his means would afford.

But during the time a very distressing problem arose
—that is, distressing for good people who have the happiness of others at heart. Tip, the colored body-servant of
the visiting minister, had fallen desperately in love with
one of Mr. Higginbotham's negro women. Tip begged
that he might be purchased by the master of the woman
he loved. It would break his heart to leave now. Brother
Murrell himself saw that it would; his soft heart was
touched deeply at the sight of such true love. So rather
than destroy such pure affection by tearing Tip away from
the only girl the boy had ever loved, the good master allowed himself to be persuaded to part with his favorite
servant. Seven hundred dollars sealed the trade, and
supposedly Tip's happiness. And then Brother Murrell
departed alone for an assumed residence.

That very night, poor Tip had his night of happiness
ruthlessly destroyed. He was rushed away, right out of
the arms of his love, by a negro-thief. But the groom was
not heartbroken, only annoyed because the "thief" had disturbed him so early. Tip was a member of Brother Murrell's evangelical band. In fact he was one of the leader's
most trusted men. He had a most important part in his
master's program, for at this time his chief source of in-
come was slave stealing. Tip had no objections to his job.
What romantic young negro would? His only duty was
to fall in love with the best looking colored girl belonging
to the richest planter in every neighborhood where the
troup held a meeting, report his predicament to the kind
master, and let him handle it. The negro-thief was also
an associate of Murrell's. Every man to his own duties!

While Brother Higginbotham was rushing about inquiring for his negro, another meeting was getting under
way in a distant community, and Tip was about his business courting another prospective wife.

Tip paid for his sins.   He knew only part of his master's plans.   That his master, who was so generous as to provide a handsome new wife for him in every community that they visited, could mean anything except good was beyond the black lover's simple reasoning.   His grand succession of honeymoons was coming to a sad close.   All might have been well, but Brother Murrell was bringing his revival campaign to a close.   He planned to go back to his home in Tennessee.   When Tip was removed from the plantation of a tender-hearted Arkansas widow who had bought him for love's sake, he experienced no regret in leaving his charming negress.   The union had lasted nearly a week.   It was probably growing tiresome anyway. He knew his master was headed for Tennessee, and he had heard that the gals over there were fat and pretty. But Tip never met any of those handsome Tennessee women who had been so highly recommended.   The dashing young swain of color was to add no more to his long list of embarrassed widows.   His usefulness as a perpetually repeating bridegroom was at an end.   He had been sold too many times already.   Descriptions of him were being posted.   It would not do good to Brother Murrell's reputation to be found with this popular negro lover in his possession.   So Tip was not allowed to go into Tennessee.   Instead he was conducted to a swamp on the Arkansas side of the Mississippi River, where he was pledged to eternal secrecy by receiving a charge of buckshot.   As his riddled body sank slowly out of sight in the black water of the swamp, the discarded bridegroom passed forever out of reach of all pursuers "for his carcass has fed many a tortoise and catfish before this time; and the frogs have sung this many a long day to the silent repose of his skeleton."

The black Don Juan having been properly disposed of, Brother Murrell set out directly for Tennessee.

On his revival tour the Reverend Murrell visited some of the outstanding towns of the country: Lexington, Kentucky; Richmond, Virginia; Charleston, South Carolina; Savannah and Augusta, Georgia. At the end of the campaign the Reverend Doctor Murrell summed up his report as follows:

"In all the route I only robbed eleven men, but I preached some mighty fine sermons, saved a good many souls, and scattered a good deal of counterfeit United States paper money among the brethren."

From an old Wood Cut

ROBBERY SCENE ALONG THE WILDERNESS TRACE (1835)

CHAPTER VI

THE FREE STATE OF SABINE

BACK in Tennessee, Murrell found that the old home country was being settled rapidly. It made him nervous to see these changes; opportunities were not so plentiful as they once were.

But Murrell, in his travels, had found a strange new country where "speculations" were plentiful and law was unknown. At first the place had offered him no great inspiration. He merely dashed into it for excitement and adventure, and after filling his pockets passed on. Now, the sight of rapid developments in his home state gave him the urge to move on. He felt cramped and hemmed in here. He began to think of better and more isolated headquarters. His thoughts turned to the Free State of Sabine.

The Free State of Sabine was a freak nation that lay along the eastern side of the Sabine River on the western border of Spanish territory. It was a bastard state that owed no nation homage, and held the respect of none. It was ruled entirely by outlaws, and there was no law except the law of might. Because of its stragetic location, it was one of the most talked of places on the continent, as well as the most feared. Practically all traffic in and out of the Southwest had to pass through this country.

And because of the immensity of this traffic and the rich-
ness of the cargoes, the outlaw realm became powerful and
wealthy, and consequently audacious.

This country was not large, not more than fifty miles
wide, with indefinite boundaries on the north and south-
east, and no military fortification. A small army could
have wiped it off the map. But in spite of the fact that
it threatened the very existence of traffic between two
important nations and held progress at a standstill along
its frontiers, no nation molested it; and its barbarous prac-
tices continued until the very name of the place became a
word of horror.

Only a strange history in a strange land could have
given birth to such a geographical freak. And only a
feverish, deep-seated international jealousy would have
permitted the existence of such a state.

The history behind the Free State of Sabine dates
back almost to Columbus' discovery of America. For it
was not long after this event that the French and Spanish
came into conflict over land in the western hemisphere.

In the year 1685 an unusual flare of jealousy broke
out among the Spaniards. In that year LaSalle, through
mistake, missed the mouth of the Mississippi River and
landed on the southern coast of Texas. The Spaniards
could not accept this extended westward cruise as an accident. They immediately renewed their efforts to colonize
Texas. And the French took advantage of LaSalle's bad
navigation and laid claim to the Texas territory. But
neither nation made any headway colonizing the territory.
Texas was too far from their bases of supplies.

After an official flurry and a lot of talk about "what
they would do," the Spaniards relaxed. LaSalle had been
murdered; and his followers had starved to death or disappeared otherwise. They forgot about Texas.

Then in 1714 they flew into another fit of jealousy.
For in that year a young French merchant by the name
of Louis Juchereau de St. Denis appeared at the presidio
of San Juan Bautista on the Rio Grande with a cargo of
merchandise to peddle. Such audacity was unheard of!
Spanish officials went into a hysterical trance over the affair. This brazen, intrusive Frenchman might find their
mines; he might call himself an explorer; he might start
France to talking about that old LaSalle claim. He was
detained at the presidio until the officers became rational
enough to decide what to do with him. Then his goods
were confiscated and he was rushed off to prison in Mexico
City.

And there one of the queerest turns of history took
place. St. Denis won the confidence of the officials,
headed an expedition of Spaniards organized to settle the
eastern frontier, and on the way back, at San Juan Bautista, recovered his goods and as an added flourish, picked
up the beautiful granddaughter of the commandant for his
wife.

St. Denis led the Spaniards to within fifteen miles of
Natchitoches, the French outpost. Here they established
the town of Los Adaes, which in time became the capital
of the Texas province. It was a puzzling act, this Frenchman leading foreigners into territory claimed by his own
country. But Louisiana at that time was a commercial
colony, and St. Denis' orders were to establish trade. It
was much easier to trade with Spaniards if they were
close to the French storehouses. Commercially and social-
ly the arrangement was satisfactory enough, but from a
diplomatic standpoint there was no end to the trouble it
brought.

Boundary disputes raged for years. In desperation,
and then in boldness Spain would claim the whole of both

Texas and Louisiana. But France too knew how to play this ancient diplomatic game. When her move came she would retaliate by claiming for herself all of Louisiana and Texas.

When the United States came into possession of Louisiana in 1803, nothing had been done about a western boundary except a lot of writing and swearing. The United States politely took up the boundary argument. But it soon became no more polite than international diplomacy forced it to be. When the diplomats failed, the armies were called in. The United States was not sufficiently patient to wait with the hope that perhaps another hundred years would in some natural way fix a boundary.

Spain let it be known that she was prepared to defend her territorial claim. The United States republic, now flushed with territory by the Louisiana Purchase, with a characteristic youthful pride, and aggravated by growing pains, gave the impression that it was ready to take on all comers. And so in the fall of 1806, both nations playing a bold part, and not to be outdone by the other, sent their armies marching viciously toward the disputed territory.

The Spanish army drew up at the west bank of the Sabine River. The American troop camped on the other bank. Soldiers on both sides stood in readiness with loaded guns waiting for the command to fire. But the command never came.

The two opposite generals got together and temporarily settled the matter by agreeing that the territory between the Sabine and the Arroyo Hondo should be neutral ground. Their respective governments ratified the treaty. And in this manner both nations saved their faces without going to war.

But little did either nation realize the outcome of such

an arrangement. A strict provision of the treaty declared that neither nation should send any armed forces into the neutral zone; no police power of any nature was provided for.

It seemed that geography had gone mad. For here, in an already unruly region where two wild frontiers met, was established a sanctuary for all those who hated law and order. No flag waved over this "No Man's Land;" no law was binding. Soon the riff-raff of the earth came pouring in, outcasts of all countries, fugitives from justice, thieves, robbers, desperadoes of all varieties. It was an outlaws' Utopia. For once within the bounds of this neutral zone, he was free of pursuit. No law could touch him here; he might laugh at all laws.

It was a desperate, reckless crew that flocked here for protection, and to live upon the commerce that passed through their state. They robbed and pillaged and murdered to their hearts' content, and preyed upon one another as wild beasts that know no law. They made capital of the jealous dispute between Spain and the United States, and dared anyone to molest them. Of great importance to the prosperity of the outlaws was the fact that the two main highways of the Southwest crossed the Neutral Ground.

What the Natchez Trace was to the Mississippi Valley, the San Antonio Trace* was to the Southwest. It was the road that St. Denis had established on his first trip to Mexico; and it immediately had become the most important highway of the Southwest. It ran from Natchitoches westward toward Mexico City directly across the Neutral Ground, a most unfortunate circumstance for travelers and traders.

---

*Often referred to as El Camino Real.

The other road was Nolan's Trace, a branch of the San Antonio Trace that left the older highway just east of the Sabine and crossed the Red River a short distance above the present city of Alexandria. Nolan's Trace was the shortest route from the western plains to the eastern stock market, and during the first half of the nineteenth century thousands of head of horses and cattle were driven over this trail.

There was no route around the Neutral Ground, and it pleased the freebooters to think of the fact.

The longer Murrell thought about the Free State of Sabine the more appealing it became to him. There in the Neutral Ground, an outlaw empire might be established. A shrewd man might become king! The thought set his ambition on edge.

So the Reverend Murrell discarded his Bible and long coat. He bought an extra pistol instead. Then he headed toward the Sabine with fantastic dreams blazing in his head.

Between the San Antonio and Nolan's traces he established himself. His headquarters were a natural marvel. No bandit could have picked a better location. His hideaway was a huge cave near the foot of the highest hill in the region. For miles on all sides open forests of virgin pines spread out in a beautiful, though confusing monotony. Occasionally there was a ravine with its stream of clear water, lined in places with small hardwood trees. But for the most part the country was a meaningless expanse of twisting, pine-covered hills. It was a confusing country to the stranger trying to find his way about.

The cave was an exceedingly large one. It served not only as living quarters, but was sufficiently large to house supplies and stable a large number of horses. A clear rippling spring branch rushed by within a few yards of the entrance. It was a beautiful, isolated, melancholy retreat where the wind forever moaned weirdly and mysteriously among the top of the tall pines.

Before long Murrell had a collection of men around him, bold, deadly ruffians who would rob or kill at the command. The cave became a treasure house. For it was the heyday of the traces. Out of the Southwest came pack-trains of silver from the Mexican mines, long droves of cattle and horses from the Texas plains, and back toward the west traveled merchants from Natchitoches, New Orleans, and Europe with their packs of silks and jewels. Many adventurers and home-seekers from the East, lured by accounts of rich lands and opportunities in Texas, headed through the Free State with high hopes, and fortune in pocket.

Murrell knew how to handle these travelers. He had outposts along the traces at strategic points — at Natchitoches, at the inns, and at the river crossings. His scouts kept him informed upon all the important business along the traces. These aids were men of various professions, inn-keepers, stock raisers, muleteers, farmers, traders. Many, perhaps most of them, did not know the extent of the workings of the gang they served. They did their small part, received their rewards, asked no questions, and kept their mouths hushed. A few became involved, more or less innocently, with Murrell, and were then afraid to turn back. It seems that for a number of years Murrell was the ruling spirit in the Neutral Ground.

It was along Nolan's Trace that Murrell committed his greatest depredations. It seemed that a curse hung over this road and those who traveled it from the time it was blazed until it faded out of use. Drama, tragedy, and romance marked the old road all the days of its impetuous life.

Philip Nolan, the man who laid out the trail, was a handsome, adventurous, young Irishman, who resided at Natchez on the eastern edge of Spanish territory. His business was dealing in horses. The Spanish army needed horses, and the animals were scarce around Natchez. Nolan saw a business opportunity and made capital of it. For a number of years he rounded up horses from the Texas plains and sold them to the officials of the Spanish dominion. It was over this road that he ran hundreds of galloping wild ponies, and in the doing accumulated a modest fortune.

But the Spaniards became suspicious about the information this American was accumulating concerning the province of Texas. While herding horses in Texas he was shot by the Spaniards, who reported to his bride of a few weeks that he had merely deserted her and his country. And then, to add misery to misfortune, a certain Edward E. Hale wrote a little book which he called *The Man Without a Country*, and through an unfortunate coincident he named his leading man Philip Nolan. And due to the circumstances and erroneous reports (later clarified by a companion of Nolan who after twenty years in Mexican prisons escaped and gave the true story) about Nolan, many believed that the American trail blazer was the young lieutenant in the Reverend Hale's book.*

Nolan's Trace, like its blazer, was destined through all its days, to a turbulent, eventful existence. Due to its remoteness it was always a dangerous road.

---

*Reverend Hale regretted this misleading circumstance; and to prove that it was all a coincidence and that he meant no injustice to the memory of Philip Nolan, he wrote another book about the real Philip Nolan and titled it **Philip Nolan's Friends.**

Before Murrell came to the Free State outlaws had from time to time stampeded droves of horses and cattle along the traces and carried them off to markets of their own selection. It had been rather easy in the matted undergrowth and canebreaks along the winding creeks. The outlaws usually knew the country better than did the drivers. And they knew how to hold their advantage. Occasionally the drivers offered resistance, but usually after a few shots they stampeded as easily as the cattle and wild horses. But Murrell had a better plan. He watched the long droves of stock go by on the way to market. Murrell had patience. These men would be back. "Why," he reasoned, "should he trouble himself to drive these stubborn wild beasts for days over wilderness roads and fight the dust and flies at their heels?" Why run any risk of complications at the market place? His prospective victims enjoyed the job too much themselves. It would grieve him much to deprive them of the pleasure! True, they would spend part of their earnings in the towns. But there was always plenty. And if the correct time and place was chosen by a specialist, the task of collecting the stock money was a frivolous detail.

Murrell planned his work with the precision of an architect. He arranged his procedure to fit the circumstance; his knack for calculating was remarkable. If an attractive drove of cattle crossed the Sabine River on the way to market, some of his men were usually on hand to investigate the matter. It was a popular procedure for some member of the gang to "accidentally" fall into company with the cow drivers and find out their business — where they expected to sell their stock, what such cattle were expected to bring at the market at that time, when they would be coming back, by what route. It was all very casual; travelers on long journeys have to talk about something. Men who talked too freely usually never lived to warn others.

After the stagecoaches started running across this country, the outlaws attacked many of them and staged bold and merciless holdups. But Murrell never made a practice of this type of robbery. It was too difficult to do away with a stage coach and an entire crew. These coaches ran on a schedule, and the disappearance of one would have been rather conspicuous. Murrell was too shrewd to run such risks. Usually he found that it was not necessary to run risks in the Neutral Ground.

If prosperous looking gentlemen were passing through No Man's Land, scouts, as a rule, spotted them. There were stops along the trace that the stages had to make. At any of these places some member of the gang might fall into conversation with a rich traveler, suggest a drink of water, or perhaps something stronger. Any scheme to get the traveler out of sight. Once this was accomplished, the rest was easy. He was killed, his possessions taken, and the robber disappeared into the forest before anyone could know that anything unusual had happened. If a traveler appeared to be a good prize, or likely to be hard to handle, a member of the gang might engage transportation over the route to see that plans were not frustrated. In some crowded inn they might be forced to sleep together. Any circumstance that necessitated privacy was arrangement enough.

On one occasion one of Murrell's scouts reported that a "rich prize" was in transit to Texas. He had stayed for awhile at the scout's inn and had made himself very impressive by telling of his wealth. A "companion" was immediately dispatched to accompany him. Shortly after dark the stagecoach drew up at a small inn that the passengers might refresh themselves and new horses might be hitched to the stage. When the impressive traveler entered the inn his "companion" and two other men, who appeared as if from nowhere, followed closely behind him. They unceremoniously rushed him into a side room. The door flew closed. A muffled scream was heard. When someone finally ventured into the room, no one was to be found. The back door was open, and outside all was quiet and apparently peaceful. When the alarm had been spread and preparation for pursuit made, it was discovered that all the horses in the corral had been turned out, and not even the stage horses could be found. The next morning the supposedly rich man's body was found in the well back of the house.

The San Antonio Trace was much older, better known, and traveled more than Nolan's Trace. There were a few villages on it, and alongside it, or near, were farmhouses. It was for over a century the most important highway west of the Mississippi.

During the heyday of the Free State of Sabine the population along the trace reached the lowest ebb in many years. Several years before the signing of the neutral zone treaty the Spanish had abandoned their capital at Los Adaes. And when war had seemed likely between the United States and Spain, most of the remaining Spaniards immigrated further into Texas or Mexico. After the outlaws took charge, only a small part of the old population remained — a few stubborn Spaniards, unconcerned half breeds, half-wild French traders, and a sprinkling of Anglo-Saxons who had established homes and dared to stay there and live in spite of the fact that no government existed. Before long citizens and traveling merchants were pleading for police protection. They had been left to a cruel fate.

When conditions had become almost intolerable, the United States government took it upon itself to clean up this nest of outlaws and thugs. But the United States was quickly warned by Spain that it was strictly against the provisions of the treaty of 1806 for any armed Americans to enter this territory, and that any such act would be construed as a hostile move toward Spain and an attempt to invade Spanish territory. The Americans had made a reputation for pushing over frontiers. And Spaniards were not inclined to take any unnecessary chances with the aggressive Americans. They were determined that they should come no closer to Spanish territory than the eastern boundary of the neutral zone. And so conditions became steadily worse in the Neutral Ground. It was perhaps the most dangerous strip of territory on the continent. Helpless people there continued to be robbed and murdered, and worse still, these marauders became so bold they made raids upon surrounding territory and then dashed back into their reserve. If the bandit could escape over the boundary of the Free State, he was safe from all punishment.

Further alarmed by this growing menace, the United States government proposed a joint campaign against the outlaws. But Spain did not choose to accept the offer. Apparently she was jealous of all moves the Americans might make, and she felt that this outlaw empire might serve as a buffer state against future aggressions.

In 1819 Spain recognized the Sabine River as her eastern boundary. And the Neutral Ground might technically have come to an end at that time. But for two years Spain refused to ratify the treaty in an effort to induce the United States not to recognize her rebellious colonies. However, in 1821 Mexico won her independence from Spain, and the United States then had Mexico to deal

with instead of Spain.   Again it seemed that the old problem would be settled and the terrible Neutral Ground
brought to an end, but the new Mexican republic, ambitious
as a result of her accomplishments, refused to recognize
the treaty made by the mother country.

The marauders continued their depredations while
diplomats at the capital cities politely argued over the
boundary question, and discussed lengthy plans, which resulted in nothing.

After 1821 the United States ventured to strengthen
her claim to the Sabine River by sending Zachary Taylor
into the disputed territory with orders to establish a fort
and look after the interests of the United States there.   In
1822 Taylor esablished Fort Jesup on the San Antonio
Trace on the watershed between the Red and Sabine rivers, about twenty miles from the latter.   The chief duties
of the troops were to guard the border, and to impress
Mexico with the strength of the United States.   And
though the country was not officially recognized as American soil, the presence of the army gave a rather definite
impression that it was only a matter of time until the Free
State of Sabine would become a part of the American commonwealth.*

Murrell did not care to become involved with soldiers.
And for that reason he confined most of his plundering to
the trace to the south.   But there was one place along
the San Antonio Trace that was too tempting for any adventurer of Murrell's caliber to miss.   That was Shawneetown, located on the trace three miles west of Fort Jesup.

The United States government in the very early days
of Fort Jesup passed a law preventing whiskey being sold

* This boundary problem was not officially settled until 1836
when Texas became an Anglo-Saxon republic.

within three miles of the flag post of the cantonment. Shawneetown sprang up at the three-mile limit. Anything the government prohibited at Fort Jesup, Shawneetown took pride in furnishing. Liquor, women, gambling, entertainment of all shades. There was open house all time.

Shawneetown was one place along the San Antonio Trace that was equipped to entertain the toughest traveler. It was the most wicked resort along the entire trace; the village boasted of the fact, and travelers advertised it well. It was a place where the mightiest made the rules and the weaker obeyed. It was the place where East and West met. To the Anglo-Saxon on his way west it was the jumping-off place; to the Latin on his way to the United States it was his introduction to the so-called civilization of the East. Many men spent their last night on earth there. Fortunes changed hands rapidly. It went on from day to day. Men shuffled dirty, limp cards over rough table tops and lost their fortunes in the doing, and then rode off over the same road that brought them, more desperate than ever.

The code of the frontier ruled. It was not a very definite thing, but strange acts were done in the name of it. Gunfire turned over-ambitious gamblers into unidentified corpses. The sound of cracking pistols, a shuffle of chairs, the pounding of galloping hoofs, another mess for the proprietor to clean up. No one seemed to bother greatly. New adventurers came, had their sprees, and yesterdays were forgotten or became heroic stories for stimulated minds to relate. It was a place where men got by on their toughness.

The place was about as far west as white women without family protection went. When the soldiers came, they flocked nearby. Men bargained for them, fought over them, cursed them and left them to their trade. No decent woman ventured near Shawneetown.

Many languages were spoken here, French, Spanish, English and half a dozen other European tongues; and then there was always the Shawnee Indians with their barbaric babble; they acted as servants, and watched the strange, mysterious drama that took place, and drew their own opinions about the pale-face civilization. It was a motley crew that visited Shawneetown: teamsters along the trace, soldiers from the fort, horse traders, horse rustlers, merchants, land prospectors, professional gamblers, outlaws, vagabonds, travelers extraordinary, adventurers in general. It was a place where the high and the low gathered, and dignity and vulgarity met with joined hands.

Shawneetown was too attractive a temptation for any young blade with an adventurous nature to miss. Here Murrell met kindred spirits. He enjoyed the society there, and spent his easy money with the entertainers; but he always had his eyes and ears open. Here was an excellent place to gossip. Travelers brought tidings from all parts. If citizens or officials were getting suspicious it would surely be talked at this place sooner or later. Murrell was a scientist in his own way. He had a mission; and he seems never to have lost sight of it. He had his frolics and his sprees, and at times he let his passion for counting other people's money get the best of his better judgment, but the man was never fickle in his purpose. From the resorts at Shawneetown the outlaw and his confederates could watch the traffic go by and calculate upon its possibilities. But to the people in the little frontier village Murrell was just another sucker, spending money recklessly. He was too shrewd to attempt any crimes near the fort. Nobody suspected Murrell because of his money. He had the bearing of a man of wealth. No one questioned these things at Shawneetown anyway.

"Business" around Fort Jesup was left to an associate gang. Not a great deal was known about the associate gangs of Murrell, or just what kind of an outlaw confederacy existed in No Man's Land, but there were several minor gangs over which Murrell exercised some control. What the system of organization was, just what allegiance the lesser chiefs held for the outlaw king, has never been determined. But in their own mysterious way they had their codes and rules.

Perhaps the boldest of Murrell's lieutenants in the Free State was Hiram Midkiff, the leader of a band of horse thieves. The Free State had been ideal for the horse rustler. Horse stealing had been one of the most thriving businesses of the district. Horses were stolen in Texas and run into the Neutral Ground, from which place they might be taken with ease to any more eastern market that might suit the convenience of the thieves. It often happened that horses were stolen in Texas, sold in the Neutral Ground, re-stolen and carried back to Texas for re-sale. It was a racket that the professional horse stealers perfected to a system.

Hiram Midkiff lived a double life. In many ways he resembled Murrell. Midkiff posed as a horse trader. On the commissary porch at Fort Jesup he whittled sticks, chewed tobacco, and swapped yarns with the officers of the fort and citizens of the community, and carried on as a regular fellow. His extensive riding about the country became noticeable, but no one could pin anything definite on him. Such were the habits of the old time horse trader.

But for a long time he was under suspicion, and citizens in their frontier way referred to him as a dangerous man. But no one ventured to make an accusation; it was considered best to be polite to him. And through fear the horse rustler commanded a great deal of respect.

Midkiff played a bold part, and his success seems to have given him too much confidence. The beginning of the end came in a rather blunt manner. One day a slave belonging to Henry Stoker, a pioneer of the Fort Jesup community, came to his master and remarked in a distressed manner that Midkiff "said for me to bring him the horse, but I'm not going to do it." It was so sudden that Stoker was puzzled for a moment. But upon a minute's reflection he sensed the plot. He questioned the negro and found that the horse thief had planned for the negro to bring his master's best horse to him in the woods.

Stoker ordered the negro to lead the horse to the spot that Midkiff had designated. It was learned that the negro was to whistle as a signal to Midkiff. Stoker ordered his negro to carry out the instructions exactly as Midkiff had given them to him, but instructed him to get out of the way just as soon as he handed him the reins.

Early that night Stoker went to the spot where his horse was to be delivered and hid nearby behind a log. He had with him two sons and two neighbor boys, whom he also stationed nearby.

Later in the night the slave came with the horse and whistled his signal at the designated spot. Midkiff appeared immediately, his rifle across his arm, cocked. Stoker shouted at him to halt. No sooner said than Midkiff's rifle cracked. Stoker, already in a squatting position, fell over backwards, just as the bullet whizzed over his head. Stoker then aimed quickly and fired. The bullet took effect in Midkiff's right breast.

Stoker and his boys set out for Fort Jesup with Midkiff, who struggled desperately every step of the way to escape. They noticed him making strained movements with his right arm. And if Stoker's bullet had not handicapped the arm, serious consequences might have resulted in the dark. For on his left shoulder was found a scabbard containing a long knife. When he had attempted to reach the knife with his left hand, the movement was so awkward that the weapon was discovered before he got his hand on it.

Midkiff was sullen. Long into the following day the citizens worked with the horse thief, questioning him. But he refused to talk.

Finally General Twiggs, an officer stationed at Fort Jesup, brought the questioning to a close. He threw a rope around Midkiff's neck and said: "We'll make him talk."

The weakening thief insisted that if they would promise to give him his freedom he would tell everything, and assured them that they would never be bothered with him again. He explained that after talking he would be forced to leave the country or his own men would kill him. Whether the men at Fort Jesup, seeing that he was dying, made the promise, or whether he volunteered, or in his delirium told, enough was learned for a posse to find his camp.

On a small creek, near the present town of Fisher, Louisiana, the posse located his camp that night. Midkiff had excellent headquarters for an outlaw. To the east were the great open forests of virgin pines; and to the west, extending to the Sabine River, were ridges of beech and oak with their thick undergrowth. It was an unsettled, broken country of hills and winding creeks and bottoms. And nearer the Sabine River was a wilderness of swamps and canebreaks, a refuge for any fleeing bandit.

Shortly after dark the posse surrounded his camp. All night they waited silently in the undergrowth near the house. Early next morning one of the men, known as Tiger Bill, came out of the house to get firewood. He saw

the men, wheeled and dashed madly toward the house.
But a bullet dropped him before he reached the door. The
bullet took effect at the point where his suspenders crossed.
His back was broken. He fell to the ground face down,
wiggling like a snake, yet struggling to make it to the
house. And it was Midkiff's own rifle that had fired.

Four or five other men were captured. When the
posse returned to Fort Jesup Midkiff was dead. Whether
the capture included all of the Midkiff band or not was
not known. But it definitely broke up horse stealing around
the fort.

Murrell personally did not dabble much with horse
stealing in the Free State. He was beginning to design
bigger things.

Ideal as the location was for the outlaw, it was not
sufficient to hold Murrell for a great length of time. He
had enough foresight to realize that sooner or later international difficulties would be cleared, and the outlaw empire would be rubbed out. Though an excellent place for
the freebooter, it was, after all, a rather small place. Murrell was always scouting for something better, something
bigger.

In the Free State of Sabine Murrell heard much talk
of the marvelous opportunities of the Spanish Territory
to the west, a land described as rich, and sure to become
the most prosperous part of the continent. It was still unsettled and only party civilized, but no one could calculate
the great wealth that lay hidden there. Fabulous fortunes
would be amassed there as if by magic!

Now that soldiers had marched into his Happy Hunting Ground, and his men were being shot down, he decided to look about for better territory. So he crossed the
Sabine and set out for the Spanish Territory to see what
there was to those fantastic tales he had been hearing.

CHAPTER VII

JOHN A. MURRELL, M. D.

JUST what Murrell thought of the Texas Country never became a matter of record. But he must have considered it favorable for speculations. For he sent for his old friend Crenshaw.

Murrell had decided to go into the underground railway business.

At that time the Abolitionists were crying for the freedom of the slaves, and societies were being organized for their liberation. Why then should anyone be looked upon with suspicion who would set out to better the condition of these unfortunate black people? There were many who would praise him. Prominent New Englanders had already gone so far as to suggest the justice as well as possible success of a general concerted action of the blacks against their white tyrants. Newspapers were established to spread propaganda. Many pious Northerners looked upon the stealing of a slave and carrying him to freedom as a religious act.

Whether or not the late Methodist evangelist looked upon the stealing of a bondaged black as the Lord's will was no great question. But he took advantage of the Abolition uproar, and for a while the evangelist became one of the most fervent disciples of the movement.

This was not the big work that Murrell was looking forward to. But he was getting closer to his idea. It

fired his ambition to do things on a large scale. Perhaps
some day he could organize the negroes into a great black
army, with his outlaw friends as officers. Such plundering as might be done! He might establish an outlaw kingdom, something like the Neutral Ground, only bigger, and
with one strong ruler. It was a crazy scheme, so mad
that even Murrell would not tell his closest associate of it.
He would wait until he knew the name of every man in
the South who would go into such a speculation, until an
organization could be perfected, until great sums of money
could be taken and stored away. But he was always hinting something spectacular, something that sounded big to
the outlaws. Murrell knew how to inspire them. He had
the ability to organize them. And no one knew this better
than Murrell himself. The underground railway Murrell
considered a definite step toward his greater plan.

The underground railway project was undertaken
about 1829. The plan was to establish a chain of underground stations reaching from the Mississippi valley to
Spanish territory in Texas. Murrell had sufficient ex-
perience in slave stealing. That gave him a decided advantage over the ordinary railway Abolitionist. Organization was the thing now to make slave stealing one of
the most profitable businesses of all time. Slaves could
be stolen in the Valley, and through the secret stations a
steady stream should pour into the Far West for sale —
not for liberation. With good organization there should
be little danger of pursuit. Prominent Abolitionists might
aid, without any knowledge of what would really happen
at the end of the route. They could be led to believe that
the company was a group of good men who wished to see
their black brothers freed from the tyranny of their white
slave masters.

When Crenshaw arrived the two talked big plans.

Crenshaw said, with a chuckle, that it was an honorable undertaking. He knew outstanding ministers in the North who were preaching constantly for this very thing. He felt that they should lend their talents to the cause. He was ready to go to work immediately.

They made a few arrangements in Texas. Then the two enthusiastic Abolitionists set out for the Valley to establish stations and look for prospective runaways.

After the project had gotten underway, it was agreed that Crenshaw would handle the sales in the Spanish territory. Murrell would remain in the Valley to secure and dispatch the black cargoes. Murrell was an expert at this art already. And at this end of the railway there should be a man who knew the law, and who was clever enough, if caught in close quarters, to appear as an Abolitionist, and not as a criminal.

It was a great plan. But there were difficulties from the very beginning. They failed to contact Abolitionists whom they could interest in the scheme. The Abolitionists raved against the Southern slave drivers and made threats and great promises. But Murrell got no money from them. Soon he was cursing them with as much vent as he cursed the aristocratic slave holders. "A bunch of noisy fools," he called them. Then there were more disappointments: many of the negroes died from hunger and exposure, some were lost, and others escaped into the forests, the Indians were always a threatening danger.

It was too risky a business. So the cherished plan for wholesale negro stealing turned out to be one of Murrell's few failures. It was definitely abandoned.

It is probable that Murrell abandoned his underground railway without giving it a more lengthy trial because of his greater idea.

Murrell was not a man to nurse failure. There was al-

ways something that he could do. He parted with Crenshaw
once more. He had decided to visit South America "and
see if there was no opening in that country for a speculation." Why might not an entire nation be enlisted in a
plot? There were many who would like to see the negroes
freed in any manner. ". . . I had also concluded that I
could get some strong friends in that quarter to aid me
in my designs relative to a negro rebellion."

The starting point of the South America expedition,
so far as the records show, was in middle Tennessee, near
a place known as Mill's Point. Murrell could never overcome the temptation of running off a choice slave. So he
began his trip by decoying a negro man from his master
and sending him by a young associate to Mill's Point.
Murrell waited behind to observe the movements of the
owner. Quite the usual thing happened. The owner made
a few visits about the country inquiring of his negro. He
thought he had run off. Nothing could be done. After a
few days Murrell instructed a friend to carry the slave
to the mouth of the Red River, which was promptly done.
Murrell took passage on a steamboat, picked up his negro
at the mouth of the Red River, and proceeded by land toward the Spanish territory. To a Louisiana planter he
sold the negro for nine hundred dollars, and two nights
later stole him again. Another friend, apparently one of
the Neutral Ground gang, ran him to the Irish Bayou
across the Texas line. Murrell followed on and sold the
negro again, this time for five hundred dollars.

It is not known how far Murrell traveled into the
Spanish countries, or how long he tarried with his prospective Latin friends. Nor is there any positive proof
that he ever visited South America. "I then resolved to
visit South America." But Murrell never made a postitive

statement to the effect that he was ever on the South
American continent, and there are no records to clarify
the question. Whether or not Murrell traveled extensively
in the Spanish countries, he stayed long enough to decide
that the Spanish would not be worth anything to him in
his plan for a rebellion. They were constantly talking
revolution at the time, but their views on the subject were
quite different from his. "Of all the people in the world,
the Spaniards are the most treacherous and cowardly;
I never want them concerned in any manner with me;
I had rather take the negroes in this country to fight than
a Spaniard."

Back in Texas Murrell continued to hear exciting talk
of interesting doings and intriguing possibilities in the
province. There might be revolutions, and in that event
a smart bandit might plunder the country to his heart's
content in the name of war. Afterward there would likely
be weak and fickle government, and easy graft. The South
American colonies were already revolting. No one could
tell what might happen in Texas. Murrell decided to wait
and look around.

He heard of rich mines and great veins of silver, cargoes from which should make easy loots. But he failed
to find them or else they were too strongly guarded for
him to rob. When he talked about what might happen to
these treasure caravans, the Spaniards became suspicious.
He failed to enlist any confederates who were bold enough
to join him. He continued to call them cowards. Murrell
made up his mind to stay on, anyway. He did not want to
miss the fun if things opened up in Texas. But he changed
his tactics.

One sunny day John A. Murrell knocked at the home
of a Catholic priest in a new part of Texas. The priest

in his best hospitality invited the well-dressed traveler into
his house. Soon the two were talking cheerfully over re-
freshments. The father was charmed by this elegant man
with polished manners who represented himself as a med-
ical doctor from the United States. It was not long before
the priest asked Dr. Murrell why he did not remain in that
community. Doctors were scarce in that country, and the
good father's people had long needed a doctor to care for
their sick.

It was after considerable persuasion on the part of
the priest that Dr. Murrell announced that he would stay.
He might as well be there as elsewhere, if the people needed
him. He had left his home in the United States through
philanthropic motives anyway.

And so the ex-evangelist outlaw became a practicing
physician in the Mexican state of Texas. The priest was
very happy; he insisted at length that the doctor take
lodging at his house. The doctor decided he could do no
better, and accepted the offer.

"I could ape the doctor first rate, having read Ewel
and several other works on primitive medicine." The
doctor became a great favorite of the priest. "He adopted
me as his son in the faith, and introduced me to all the
best families as a young doctor from North America."

Before the young doctor had been with the priest
long, he became "a great Roman Catholic, and bowed to
the cross, and attended regularly to all the ceremonies of
that persuasion." He later commented: "All the Catholic
requires or needs to be universally received is to be correctly represented."

Murrell soon built up a heavy practice. Seemingly
he might have been a successful doctor. But the profession
was too dull for a man of his restless nature. Office work
bored him, and he was annoyed because the revolution was

making no noticeable progress. In the course of his practice the doctor discovered the good man's treasure. To him that discovery was much more interesting than locating the cause of a stomach-ache, and immediately his interest in healing began to decline. The practitioner's thoughts began to dwell more in the field of surgery.

His career as a physician came to a crowning climax one afternoon when he and the priest's secretary were alone in the house. The doctor turned surgeon, and after making cautious preparations, though without formal examination of his patient, performed his last operation, in that capacity, upon the priest's secretary. It was a throat operation from which the patient never recovered. It was a neat job, the work of a specialist. Two swift strokes of Dr. Murrell's operating knife and both jugular veins were correctly severed. The family doctor had already located the treasury. So without any great inconvenience he paid himself most handsomely for his professional services and left his patient in a most unattractive position on the floor of the priest's home.

The amount of money found was nine hundred and sixty dollars in gold. ". . . And I could have got as much more in silver if I could have carried it." Murrell complained about so much of the priest's money being silver.

While Murrell was rapidly making his way toward New Orleans with his sacks of gold, the father returned home to find his community again without a physician and himself minus nine hundred and sixty gold dollars and a secretary.

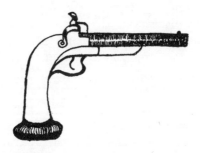

CHAPTER VIII.

REBELLION DECIDED UPON

IN New Orleans the ex-doctor called his associates together and after some "high fun with old Mother Surgick's girls," the gentlemen settled down to business. And
a ghastly business it was. Murrell had decided to spring
his secret.

Instead of stealing negroes and encouraging them to
run away, he would incite them to rebellion. He would
arouse a burning hatred for their masters. If the Abolitionists would not free the negroes, then the slaves must
take the burden upon themselves and rebel. That was part
of the general idea that Murrell wanted the slaves to get.
An hour would be set, and all the slaves would strike at
the same time. A great secret clan would be organized,
and white members would instruct and direct the negroes.
With this army of slaves striking independently but at a
given hour, the South would be thrown into such confusion
as it could not overcome before the land would be plun-
dered. Before the whites could organize, the South would
be pillaged. With his white lieutenants and black regi-

ments he would wreck revenge upon the South, and in the doing become fabulously rich.

This was Murrell's great "conspiracy" at last. It was a mad scheme at best, but it was more feasible then than now. Towns were scattered; in the plantation villages the slaves greatly outnumbered their owners; law officers were few and scattered; there were no quick means of communication. The dense swamps and wilderness would offer a means of retreat. There would be bloodshed and vengeance. That was something to think of. Then there would be fabulous riches, the life savings of rich planters.

Murrell's ambition had become almost a consuming passion. He had a mania to do something big. The outlaws listened with amazement. Some thought the man was not serious, just vainly trying to be impressive. But Murrell talked on. He was dead serious. He told them: "All the crimes I have ever committed have been of the most daring; and I have been successful in all my attempts as yet." He spoke of a crowning and inspiring future success. He worked up their vent toward society. He told of his hate: "I look on the American people as my common enemy; they have disgraced me, and they can do no more. My life shall be spent as their devoted enemy."

Mad as the scheme may have sounded, Murrell never failed to reason, and in the main he led the outlaws to agree with him.

Murrell knew, however, that the real purpose of the plot could not be told to everyone; only men who had proven their grit would be entrusted with the secret. All must proceed cautiously, very cautiously. There was no need to hurry. He knew that to attempt to execute such a plot at once would be suicide. He had no intention of hurrying. Why should he? He had already waited for years. But now he was planning, definitely.

At a friend's house the outlaws who had "proven their
grit" met. "We sat in council three days before we got
our plans to our notion; we then determined to undertake
the rebellion at every hazard." The clan was born.

Murrell's final word was that of caution. He told
of the case of Tom Phelps to illustrate his point. Phelps
was one of the men who had helped rob Murrell on one of
his earlier trips to New Orleans. The two men had become
acquainted in this manner and later friends in the business.
Phelps was arrested and put in jail in Vicksburg. Murrell felt sorry for him and wanted to help, but found him
so strictly watched that nothing could be done to free him.
"He was a noble fellow, but a weakling also," Murrell
pointed out to his friends. "He wants them (the negroes)
all free; and he knows how to excite them as well as any
person; but he will not do for a robber, as he cannot kill
a man unless he has received an injury from him first."
Phelps had been in the habit of stopping men on the highway and robbing them and letting them go on. He had
been identified by one of his victims. "That will never
do for a robber," Murrell explained emphatically. "After
I rob a man, he will never give evidence against me;
there is but one safe plan in the business, and that is to
kill. . . . If I could not afford to kill a man, I would not
rob." The men agreed.

The immediate object of the clansmen was to "make
as many friends as possible for the purpose," to find the
worth of every man who could be trusted, and then to have
them located in proper places. "We design having our
companies so stationed over the country, in the vicinity
of the banks and large cities, and when the negroes commence their carnage and slaughter, we will have detachments to fire the towns and rob the banks while all is con-

fusion and dismay."

Business attended to, the men left New Orleans and scattered over the Valley to find "friends."

Murrell set out for Natchez on foot. He had sold his horse in the city with the intention of stealing another; but on the road no immediate opportunity presented itself. It was noon of the fifth day before an opportunity came for him to get a horse. Murrell was weary and tired. He had stopped at a creek to get some water. While he was sitting on a log resting, he sighted a traveler down the road riding a fine-looking horse. "The very moment I saw him, I determined to have his horse if he was in the garb of a traveler." The horseman rode up, and it was easily seen that his equipage was that of a traveler. Murrell rose suddenly from his seat by the roadside and moved to the middle of the road, pistol in hand. The man drew rein. He tried to talk but he only babbled. Murrell beaded his elegant rifle pistol at the man's head and ordered him to dismount. He came down clumsily. Murrell took the reins, and pointing toward the creek ordered the man to walk before him. Half stiff with fright, the man stumbled on in front of the pointed pistol until the two had gone several hundred yards into the woods.

"I hitched his horse, then made him undress himself, all to his shirt and drawers, and ordered him to turn his back to me."

Then, wide-eyed with terror, the man asked if he was going to be shot. Murrell had to order him the second time to turn his back. The man asked for time to pray before he died. "I told him I had no time to hear him pray. He turned around and dropped on his knees, and I shot him through the back of the head."

The next step was to dispose of the body. Murrell knew how to do that. "I ripped open his belly and took out his entrails." In the vacant space he stuffed sand to weight the body down. Then he threw the limp corpse splashing into the creek. That matter well taken care of,

Murrell turned his attention to the man's clothes. "I then searched his pockets and found four hundred and one dollars and thirty-seven cents, and a number of papers that I did not take time to examine. I sunk the pocket-book and papers and his hat in the creek. His boots were brand new and fitted very genteely, so I put them on and sank my old shoes in the creek to atone for them."

Murrell did not misjudge the traveler's horse. It was "as fine a horse as ever I straddled." Traveling became pleasant enough.

Natchez was a great place to have a good time. Murrell had friends there. Some of them he could tell of his conspiracy. To others he could only hint things that might be done. He was eager also to make other acquaintances, bold, dissatisfied characters who would speculate, men who had nothing to lose, outcasts who hated society. Natchez was an excellent place to make such acquaintances. It was at Natchez that Murrell had found Carter, sitting in Walton's tavern-bar, quoting scripture at his "little shifty-eyed quadroon girl." Many plots had been hatched in Natchez near the water front.

Natchez had grown rapidly like a mushroom. Only a few years after the site had been cleared from the virgin wilderness it held a commanding position in trade and commerce; its beauty was outstanding, "the handsomest city in America, next to Charleston," a visitor observed.

Travelers left inspiring descriptions: "A town handsomely located on a picturesque bluff . . . highly romantic . . . extravagant in flowers . . . abundant in foliage . . . dreamy mansions, jessamine shaded . . . teeming streets . . . long columned dwellings . . . lawns with live oaks and sycamores deep with moss . . . breezes fragrant with the scent of orange blossoms from the southward . . . a city of wealth and beauty." That was Natchez that occupied the Bluff.

Under the Bluff was a different picture. Life was bitter, threatening, dangerous. Natchez, like all the larger river ports of this period, along the Mississippi, had its district branded "indecent." These were terrible, disgraceful, filthy sections, usually located along the water front, low and irregular, crowding the first banks of the Mississippi. These underworlds were considered necessary evils. It was considered better that the two classes of society should not mix.

Between the base of the cliff and the river were two narrow, congested, filthy streets, and a criss-cross of nar-

row alleys. Anything might go on here. The place was
known as one of the vice spots of America. No wonder
Murrell came here to find men of his mold. The houses
of pleasure drew the ruffians of the valley as a light at-
tracts moths. Reckless boatmen, nimble-fingered gamblers,
pick-pockets, pimps, highwaymen, gunmen, and thugs of
all varieties gathered here for the low pleasures of Natchez-under-the-Hill, to boast of their terrifying experiences, to curse society, to make new plots, to get gloriously
drunk and fight among themselves, to carry on until their
lewd appetites were satisfied. It was a reckless hell of
loose characters who fought and killed among themselves,
but were always bound together by their common hatred
for the aristocrats on the Hill.

Men swaggered from saloons to gambling halls mumbling their vulgar thoughts; women of ravaged beauty
paraded the streets in their seductive dress to be seen by
the men who kept them alive with gambled and robbed
money; it went on day and night; the section never slept.
Occasionally men passed away to the sound of cracking
revolvers. There would be a rustle along the water's edge,
the frantic scream of a woman perhaps, distracted, foul
oaths from a group of men; the tin-panny pianos in the
dance halls would stop their rhythmic, nervous beat, the
sound of scraping feet turn into a confusion. But in a
few moments the pianos would take up their jerky beat,
drinks would be circulating, the ziz-ziz of dancing feet
would be heard, coarse laughter would float out over the
river. It was all forgotten as quickly as it happened. Nobody in the town on the Hill bothered. Such things were
expected. Just another bad character out of the way. So
much the better.

In musty smoke-filled gambling-rooms professional
river gamblers with hard-lined faces met the outlaws, and

with dirty, limp cards took what the bandits gained on the traces with the gun. Over and over the outlaws would lose their looted fortunes, curse fate, and stagger out again to regain another.

Murrell soon found his friends there. "I reached Natchez and spent two days with my friends . . . and the girls under the hill." These "girls under-the-hill" swarmed; they plied their trade until the red-light district of Natchez was famous along the entire Mississippi.

A mere whisper of the news that Murrell brought to his friends under the hill would have made the town above tremble. But so long as these dregs of humanity stayed below and did not attempt to come up into the city, no one gave thought of the horrible plots and conspiracies that might be hatched there. The beautiful, peaceful town on the hill slept on.

From Natchez Murrell set out for the Choctaw nation with the intention, as he said, of giving some of them a chance for their property. Most of the Catholic priest's money had been spent by this time. Murrell had visited both New Orleans and Natchez, and either city was enough to break the purse of the average outlaw.

On the road to the Choctaw Nation he committed a robbery which he considered humorous. It proved a joke on Murrell, but he enjoyed telling of it none the less:

"As I was riding along between Benton and Rankin, planning for my designs, I was overtaken by a tall and good-looking young man on an elegant horse, splendidly rigged. The young gentleman's apparel was of the gayest that could be had, and his watch chain and other jewelry were of the richest and best. I was anxious to know if he intended to travel through the Choctaw Nation, and soon managed to learn. He said that he had been to the lower country with a drove of negroes, and was returning home to Kentucky. We rode on, and soon got very intimate for strangers, and agreed to be company through the Indian nation. We were two fine-looking men, and to hear us talk, we were very rich. I felt him on the subject of speculation, but he cursed the speculators, and said he was in a bad condition to fall into the hands of such villains; that he had the cash with him that twenty negroes had sold for. He said that he was very happy that he happened to get in company with me through the Nation.

"I concluded he was a noble prize and longed to be counting his cash. At length we came into one of those long stretches in the Nation where there was no house for twenty miles. It was the third day after we had been in company with each other. The country was high, hilly, and broken, and had no water. Just about the time I reached the place where I intended to count my companion's cash, I became very thirsty and insisted on turning down a deep hollow, or dale, that headed near the road, to hunt some water. We had followed down the dale for near four hundred yards when I drew my pistol and shot him through. He fell dead. I commenced hunting for his cash and opened his large pocket-book, which was stuffed very full. And when I began to open it, I thought it was a treasure indeed. But oh! the contents of that pocket-book! It was richly filled with copies of love songs . . . and love letters, some of his own composition — but no cash. I began to cut off his clothes with my knife and examine them for his money. I found four dollars and a half in change in his pockets and no more; and is that the amount for which twenty negroes sold? thought I. I recollected his watch and jewelry, and I gathered them. His chain was rich and good, but it was swung to an old brass watch. He was a puff for true, and I thought all such fools ought to die as soon as possible. I took his horse and swapped him to an Indian native for four ponies, and sold them on the way home."

Murrell did not find business so good in the Choctaw Nation. A few shady horse deals and he was back home for a little rest. "I reached home and spent a few weeks among the girls of my acquaintance in all the enjoyments that money could afford."

From Pictorial America

FRONTIER HOME ON THE TENNESSEE RIVER
IN MURRELL'S TIME

CHAPTER IX

SECOND EVANGELICAL CAMPAIGN

THE pleasures of the home girls did not hold Murrell for long. He was now a man with a mission. He had definite plans to execute, and they were big plans. The man was a power house of restless energy. He was constantly perfecting his plans, molding new schemes, working up his vent for society. He had comrades who would back him in anything. But he must have more, many more. He would have men in every section of the South who would obey his commands. It pleased him to think of that. Power was an idol that John A. Murrell worshipped. Some day perhaps he might be a king. Who would stop him? The law of the South had had ample opportunity and had done little. Law! It was a joke. It had stung him once. But it would never do so again. Riches should go to the mightiest. A little more time and he would show what power really could do.

Friends in the business! That was the first step. Another extensive campaign was planned, one that would cover practically the entire South. Murrell wanted to study his field of campaign. He wanted to know the worth of every valuable man in it.

Memphis was a place to find adventurous characters. Murrell had friends there already with whom he would trust his right eye. That would be a good place to start. And it was a good place to pick up some traveling expenses also.

Murrell headed south for Memphis.

Memphis had grown fast, in fact too fast for much organization. As a river port it was one of the most prosperous on the Mississippi. It was a typical Western boom town. "People made it a business every Saturday to go to town to get drunk and fight." Whiskey was cheap. Dean's best could be bought for twenty-five cents a gallon. Some who were over-fond of this favorite firewater declared that they never intended drinking water as long as they could get whiskey at that price. "They were so systematic in their carousals that the boys would beg their parents to let them go to town on Saturdays to see the fights."

The river brought its supply of reckless, tough characters. Down the Mississippi there floated a constant pageant of boats. Almost every device that could be made to float was used to ride the current of the Mississippi: heavy, ponderous barges, slender, stylish-looking keels, flatboats, pirogues, canoes, skiffs and dugouts.

On the large barges two or three families often traveled, seeking new homes, and carrying with them all household effects including poultry, produce, hogs, mules and cows. On the keels pleasure seeking parties frequently came down the river on a jaunt to New Orleans. These boats were usually fairly comfortably fixed, sometimes elaborate. There were bedrooms, a dancing room and a platform for dancing. Many of them carried gay parties. At each large village these boats landed for a few days to visit the town. Memphis was a favorite resort.

The flatboats carried a more lowly crew: the needy, the desperate, the adventurous. Upon these crude boats poor families frequently lived for months, lazily floating with the current. But more frequently the flatboats were tenanted by the rough elements of society, carrying the produce of the year's market, eager for amusement, and generally well supplied with fire-arms and whiskey.

Frequently taunts and insults were exchanged, sometimes ending in blows, pistol shots, stabs, and death. These river people were a coarse bunch who lived hard and fought hard. Like beasts they preyed upon each other; but when they tied their boats up at the wharfs and stepped off into the river ports, they instinctively banded together against the stationary element as a common enemy. The more there were of these rovers in town, the more dangerous it was. Memphis always had more than its share of these river characters.

It is said that the flatboatmen "took the town" when they liked. They paid the city fees for wharfage when it suited their pleasure, and it seldom suited them.

A typical clash occurred one day when a certain bully by the name of Trewter landed in one of his ugly moods. He had previously passed down the river, and had landed at Memphis without having to pay fee. He was considerably annoyed when he was told that the flatboatmen must pay fee. He cursed and raved and threatened. He worked the boatmen into a state of rage. He announced that he would set an example, and flashed a heavy haw stick with knots, which he said he had cut for the specific purpose of using on the wharfmaster's head. No one would make him pay fees. He was unusually bold that day, perhaps because they were about five hundred other flatboatmen at the Memphis landing.

Not caring to take any chances with his head, the wharfmaster swore out a warrant and turned the matter over to an officer, G. B. Locke by name, with orders to serve it. Whether it was the haw stick or the five hundred flatboatmen sulking along the wharfs that turned Officer Locke back was not known. But soon he came back, beating it up the hill much faster than he had gone down. The flatboatmen had "taken the town."

It was then that the city decided to set an example. A detachment of the Memphis Guards, a local military company, was sent into the river section. Seeing the uniforms and bayonets, Trewter made for the river and pushed off. He was pursued; and when overtaken he resisted violently. A bullet put a quick end to his career.

For a day it seemed that the flatboatmen would declare open war on the city. They cursed and threatened. The Pinch Gut was a swarming hive of demons. But after a while, perhaps for the want of leadership, they lost courage and sulkily slunk back into the dark pattern of the river edge section. Such events characterized the strife that existed between the two classes of society in Memphis.

What Natchez-under-the-Hill was to Natchez, the "Pinch Gut" was to Memphis. This peculiar appellation was the cause of considerable hatred between the two classes of society in the town. The uncomplimentary name was given by one section of Catfish Bay to an adjoining neighborhood, as the result of some hurrahing which occurred during the course of an athletic contest between the two factions. Some say that the term was suggested by the hungry appearance of the wives and children there, or by the "dullness of trade at the tavern, which sometimes subjected the husbands to the disagreeable necessity of going home sober." Others have said that it was because the people there pinched their guts for whiskey. Anyway, the Pinch Gut neighborhood did not like the name, and a feud started between the rivals of Catfish Bay. The feud was greatly enjoyed by those who fancied themselves out of the bounds of either district. This proved a mistake. More distant neighbors settled the dispute by dubbing the entire surroundings of Catfish Bay the "Pinch Gut." The residents of Catfish Bay hated the name, and for that reason, if for no other, they hated the upper class who referred to their homes as the "Gut."

The district spread until it threatened to take in the respectable section of the town. The place became a power; and at times there was open warfare between the respectable section and this district. Both hated the other, and for that reason, if no other, they lived to themselves.

Along the wharfs, a rowdy, tough bunch caroused: red-shirted flatboatmen, trappers in buckskin, gaudily dressed gamblers, third-rate dancers, counterfeiters, horse thieves and prostitutes. They all carried on about as they pleased in the shanties under the Bluff.

In the Pinch Gut Murrell met his friends, contacted a few new adventurous characters, and whispered to a choice few his scheme that would make them all rich, and perhaps powerful. In the shanties under the Bluff he had his fill of the filthy pleasures that the slum town afforded, and then, as from Natchez-under-the-Hill, he emerged again on the highway a pious and dignified man. Again he pressed tenderly under his arm the Holy Bible. His heart was again burdened with the lost souls of the South. He now had plans for a more extensive evangelical tour than ever before. He was surveying his field for future action. The guise of a minister suited his purpose most fittingly.

The double, contradictory life of John A. Murrell has been called one of the great human puzzles. But the frontier, during Murrell's day, presented many examples where crime and religion worked hand in hand. Murrell's duplicity, though unexcelled, was by no means singular.

The notorious highwayman, Joseph Thompson Hare, fought his companion in crime to keep them in the straight and narrow path. When they did not heed him, "I read them from John Wesley's magazine." He "preached at them to abandon the life of the highwaymen."

He had "spiritual" experiences. One night, soon after robbing a man, he saw standing across the road in front of him a beautiful white horse, "as white as snow." Upon his approach the horse disappeared suddenly. The vision made him uneasy and he stopped his flight from pursuit. The delay proved disastrous. He was captured that night. And during the five year prison term that followed, he spent his time reading the Bible and writing in his *Confessions*. "I think this white horse was Christ and that he came to warn me of my sins, and to make me fear and repent," he later said.

Within a year after his release he staged a mail coach robbery between Boston and Havre-de-Grace and made away with a loot of sixteen thousand, nine hundred dollars. Less than a week later he was back in jail reading his Bible, praying, preaching to the attendants and waiting for the trial that found him guilty of a capital offense.

He dropped his Bible and said amen to his long prayer just as the noose dropped over his head. To all appearances he died at peace "in a great hope."

The father of Jesse James, like the father of John A. Murrell, was a minister. "A mighty preacher," the Missourians called him.

When news of the gold discovery reached Missouri, the

Reverend Robert James embarked in a covered wagon for the California gold fields with a hope of gaining "a sufficient fortune to educate his children." But the Reverend James never returned. He died soon after reaching California; and the boys proceeded to educate themselves.

Jesse, while a young man, was baptized, and both he and his brother Frank were schooled in the old-fashioned religion.

In later life Jesse was met one day by an old Baptist minister who had preached to him as a boy. The minister questioned the outlaw about the things he was doing, and asked why he did not mend his ways. Jessie replied promptly that he would be glad enough to stop, but he did not intend to stop right under a rope.

The minister then insisted that Jesse should not forget his religion. He reminded the outlaw that his father had been a good man, and that Jesse himself had been brought up religiously.

The outlaw was touched by this. He thrust his hand into his inside coat pocket and produced a small book which he handed to the preacher. It was a copy of the New Testament. The minister looked through the book in astonishment. Never in his life, he related, had he seen a Bible so marked up, showing such constant usage.

Jesse James had a simple but firm religious belief. He believed in a personal God and a personal devil. The outlaw believed that he had lived the best possible life under the circumstances, and therefore was entitled to salvation. Jesse's mother testified at her son's inquest that when Jesse left her home, less than two weeks before he was killed, he said to her at parting:

"Well, mother, if I never see you again, we'll meet in Heaven."*

---

* Robertus Love, The Rise and Fall of Jesse James, PP. 32 - 36.

Cole Younger, outstanding member of the Jesse James gang, was said to have been a man with a deep religious turn. A niece, on one occasion, said to a biographer, "Uncle Cole liked to read. . . . He liked theological works. . . . You know he was always deeply interested in religion, probably would have been a minister if the war hadn't come along and changed everything for him."*

John Westley Hardin was also the son of a preacher, and he followed the paternal example so far as to study theology. Perhaps no American killer ever left an authentic record of more victims than Hardin. In his autobiography he left a list of thirty-five victims, with dates and names appended. Hardin did not necessarily kill more men than any other, doubtless not as many as Murrell; but he had a clearer record of more killings. Hardin, like Murrell, had an intellect far above the average; and, like Murrell, he also had a knack for turning his hand to various lines of work. He was not only a theologian and a killer, he was a school teacher and lawyer as well. In the penitentiary he "gave a great deal of attention to theology." He ran the prison Sunday school and was considered an authority on the Bible.

Murrell was not the only man of this period who studied the Bible and ways to kill men at the same time.

But no outlaw out-did Murrell with scripture, and perhaps few divines of the frontier excelled him as a preacher. Murrell, from the days of his youth, was a student of the Bible. He read it often and studiously; and if he did not interpret it sincerely, he interpreted it none the less eloquently and convincingly. He was a keen student, a great organizer, elegant and attractive; and he knew the nature of the backwoods people to whom he preached.

_____
* Ibid.   50 - 51.

He was nothing less than a genius. Many people were converted during his revivals, and many Christians were inspired to better living. Regardless of what frontier people may have lost through the efforts of this man, many of them gained salvation and a brighter hope.

Murrell's second evangelical tour was more extended than the first. "My next trip was through Georgia, South Carolina, North Carolina, Virginia and Maryland, and then back to South Carolina, and from there round by Florida and Alabama. . . . I began to conduct the progress of my operations and establish my emissaries over the country in every direction." He was winding in and out of the backwoods settlements, meeting his men, learning of others, stealing negroes here and there, and occasionally helping with horse stealing — a petty hobby he could never quite cast off — always moving, mysteriously appearing, and mysteriously disappearing. Even among the speculators Murrell did not represent himself always in the same manner. To some he was a great Abolitionist, a good man burning with a desire to see the toiling black people gain the freedom that God intended for them. To others he was a philosopher who saw and preached the great injustice of the aristocrats having all the good things of life while others toiled from daylight to dark and had nothing. To the hardened criminal he was an ideal, a man who was clever, powerful, who had the nerve for anything.

Through it all Murrell had to finance his plan. He was five years organizing and developing it. It was expensive business. But the Reverend Murrell had a way of taking care of these matters. He had already found that a revival meeting furnished an excellent atmosphere for his work. The arrangement suited his purpose most conveniently, and he knew how to take every advantage of such a situation.

During the hysterical shouting of camp meetings it was quite easy for horses to gallop off unheard. People lost all sense of their surroundings. And no one examined very closely the currency passed out by a transient evangelist.

No direct description of any of the revival meetings in which Brother Murrell took part have been handed down. However, numerous accounts of meetings of this period have been preserved. The meeting held in Hancock County, Georgia was somewhat typical of the larger camp meetings of Murrell's day:

The Methodists have lately had a Camp-Meeting in Hancock County, about three miles south of Sparta in Georgia. The meeting began on Tuesday, 28th July, at 12 o'clock, and ended on Saturday following. We counted thirty-seven Methodist preachers at the meeting; and with the assistance of a friend I took an account of the Tents, and there were one hundred and seventy-six of them, and many were very large. From the number of people who attended preaching at the rising of the sun, I concluded that there were about 3,000 persons, white and black to-gether, that lodged on the ground that night. I think the largest congregation was about 4,000 hearers.

We fixed the plan to preach four times a day — at sunrise, 10 o'clock, 3 o'clock and at night and in general we had an exhortation after the sermon. We had 14 sermons preached at the Stage; and 9 exhortations given after the the sermons were closed; besides these, there were two sermons preached at the Tents on one night, when it was not convenient to have preaching at the Stage.

The ground was laid out in a tolerable convenient place, containing 4 or 5 acres, and the Tents were pitched close to each other; yet the ground only admitted of about 120 Tents in the lines; the other Tents were pitched behind them in an irregular manner.

We had plenty of springs convenient to supply men and beasts with water.

The first day of the meeting, we had a gentle and comfortable moving of the spirit of the Lord among us; and at night it was much more powerful than before, and the meeting was kept up all night without intermission — however, before day the white people retired, and the meeting was continued by the black people.

On Wednesday at 10 o'clock the meeting was remarkably lively, and many souls were deeply wrought upon; and at the close of the sermon there was a general cry for mercy; and before night there were a good many persons who professed to get converted. That night the meeting continued all night both by the white and black people, and many souls were converted before day.

On Thursday the work revived more and spread farther than what it had done before; and at night there was such a general stir among the mourners at the Stage that we did not attempt to preach there; and as we had but one Stage it was best to have preaching at some of the Tents. The meeting at the Stage continued all night and several souls were brought to God before day, and some just as the day broke.

Friday night was the greatest day of all. We had the Lord's Supper at night, by candlelight, where several hundred communicants attended; three of the preachers fell helpless within the altar; and one lay a considerable time before he came to himself. From that the work of convictions and conversions spread, and a large number were converted during the night, and there was no intermission until the break of day — at that time many stout hearted sinners were conquered.

On Saturday morning we had preaching at the rising of the sun; and then with many tears we took leave of each other.

I suppose there were about eighty souls converted at that meeting, including white and black people. It is thought by many people that they never saw a better Camp-Meeting in Georgia.

The people in general behaved exceedingly well; and there was not a public reproof given from the pulpit during the meeting. There were a few disorderly persons who brought liquors to sell, &c. But the magistrates took some of them with a State warrant, and bound them over to court; after this we were more quiet.*

During the entire campaign Murrell was quietly contacting his men, directing his lieutenants in horse-stealing, passing counterfeit, stealing slaves.

Murrell was on his way home. It had been an "eventful" trip. There was one daring episode of the campaign which he especially enjoyed relating. He considered it rather funny. Even during his most cold-blooded escapades Murrell would have his joke.

"After I had turned for home from Alabama, I was passing by where one of my friends lived with three of my associates." The men stopped. On the front porch of the friend's house the men engaged in conversation. And while they were sitting there talking a large drove of sheep came up "to the blocks." The host went out and examined them and found them to be the flock of "an old Baptist" who lived five or six miles up the road. The flock had strayed from the owner some three months before. The owner had ridden about the country making inquiries about his sheep, but he heard no word of them. When he failed to find them, he accused this neighbor of driving

*Reprinted by permission of the publishers, The Arthur H. Clark Company, from Ulrich B. Phillips's "Plantation and Frontier Documents," Vol. II, pp. 284-286.

his sheep off to market. His reputation most likely was sufficient to merit suspicion. But the accused host was very indignant. He told his guests that the old man had abused him "as if he were a common thief."

It was then that Murrell decided to play a trick on the old man for his suspicions. After a brief chat about "business," he bade his host good-bye and with his three companions gathered up all the sheep and drove them on before them. They arrived at the owner's place just after dark. The travelers called the old gentleman out to the gate and asked if they might lodge with him that night. The man expressed his regrets that he could not accommodate them and urged as a reason that his "old woman" was sick.

Murrell would not be outdone. He answered that he had three active young men with him, who could do all that was wanting to be done. They could wait upon themselves. Murrell, ever ready with a good explanation, said that he had moved down below in the spring of that year, and at the time his sheep were scattered and he had concluded to leave them until fall. He was then on his way from the old place and was going to his new home. He had had a hard drive that day. Both his men and sheep were tired out. It would be considered a great favor if he would accommodate them. It was then after dark and his men were very hungry. Murrell, attempting further to put the prospective host at ease, explained that he need not worry about food, that he had a very fine wether that he wished to kill. He had been mean to drive that day, and what was not used that night, the host might have for himself.

No gentleman of the old South could have closed his doors in the faces of such complaisant visitors. He would do the very best by them that he could. He showed the strangers to a place where they could pen their sheep, and to the corn crib and stables. They might help themselves. They were welcome if they could wait upon themselves.

The nocturnal callers soon had their horses fed and the mutton dressed. The host told them where they might find meal, milk and butter. Soon a large pot of choice mutton was cooking over a roaring fire. While the associates were cooking the sheep, Murrell was conversing with the "old Baptist" on the subject of religion. Murrell represented himself as a Baptist preacher.

"When the news came that the sheep was done, I went into the kitchen and we had a real feast of mutton at the expense of the old Baptist.

"After supper we went into where the old lady lay sick. The old man got his Bible and hymn book, and invited me to go to duty. I used the books, and then prayed like hell for the recovery of the old lady."

The next morning the men arose early and had the sheep on the road before daylight. The sheep were driven about a mile, scattered in the woods, and left.

"We left the head of the wether that we killed lying in the lot, where the old man could see that it was his own mark."

The men spurred their horses toward home. They considered the joke on the old Baptist very funny.

And thus came the end of John A. Murrell's second evangelical campaign. He felt more sure of himself now. His plot was growing and taking shape. It seemed safe enough. Who would ever have suspected this pious sanctimonious minister of plotting the destruction of the entire South!

CHAPTER X

HOME LIFE

ALL of Murrell's life was not spent roving. Before the conspiracy was far under way he established a home in Madison County, Tennessee. The home was on a large farm, and according to reports, he lived in grand style. He entertained his friends "royally." His generosity, his charming manner, and engaging conversation made him a delightful host. But there was something mysterious about the man. And many both feared and respected him at the same time. His long absences from home made the neighbors wonder. But he was a wealthy man of affairs. It was quite natural that business might take such a man away from home for protracted spells. The backwoodsmen of Madison County lived much to themselves; news traveled slowly in that day. And then, wealth was a thing to attract attention; the backwoodsmen respected it blindly.

Unlike other outlaws of the period, who fought society openly and aired their hatred for all social order, Murrell was more subtle. His pride and dignity raised him above the ordinary methods. There was a deep-seated hatred that made his vengeance a consuming passion. Instead of

spurning law and society, he devoted himself to the study
of both. He lived in Madison County as an ordinary
family man, who conversed with his neighbors on the
topics of the day—farming, stock-raising, Mississippi
trade, the slave problem, and religion. He was a man
with whom people enjoyed talking. And Murrell loved
to impress the country folk with his smooth and clever
talk. His vanity was his consuming weakness—a failing
that ultimately led to his ruin.

Not a great deal was ever known about John A. Murrell's wife. Her origin, as well as her final outcome, were
both mysterious and vague. She was a shadowy figure
at best. The great outlaw spoke of her less than of his
mother. Most likely she was never a guiding force in
his life. He was a hardened criminal before he met her.
And at that stage there was doubtless little that anyone
could have done to influence him for better or worse.
Whether the woman knew of his terrible character or not,
was never known. Probably she did, and it has been
said that she was a woman with a reputation, also.

The historian, Keating, alleged that Murrell married
an Ohio girl whose name was Mary McClovey. Her
father, according to this source, was an Irish emigrant
who in 1799, married a pretty servant girl employed at
the government garrison at Cincinnati. McClovey was
for a number of years the servant of Dr. Allison, famous
as the first physician of Cincinnati, and who, for awhile,
lived between Permton and Stonelick, in Clermont, then
Hamilton County, about the year 1800. About 1810
McClovey went with Dr. Allison to Cincinnati, and in that
city the girl was reared. She was handsome and romantic, and her advantages of culture had been good; for her
father had prospered. When about eighteen the girl met

Murrell, who was in the city, probably selling stolen horses. She was infatuated with the man's dash and personal beauty. She fled with him to Lexington, where they were married, much against the wishes of her father.

Coates* stated that Murrell married a woman from the red-light district in the "Gut" at Memphis.

According to this account there was a tragedy behind the marriage. It all started while Murrell and Crenshaw were on their early trip to Alabama. Coming out of Georgia, Murrell had fallen sick. He tried to ride on anyway, but when they had crossed into Alabama he could go no further. And so the men stopped at the little town of Columbia. Murrell went to bed with a high fever.

For several days he lay tossing and mumbling in his delirium. When his burning fever left him and he came to his senses, he was weak and his body felt numb. He tried to walk, but it was impossible. He stuck to his bed for three days more. The innkeeper's daughter nursed him. She prepared appetizing dishes for him, and stayed near for his call; and the outlaw lay there helpless on his bed with his dark eyes following the attractive figure who cared for him.

Murrell said little. Even when the time came to leave he made no display. But once on the road again Crenshaw joshed him. He told Murrell that the pretty miss back at the inn had an eye for him; he had heard her tell her father that he had such genteel manners as she had never seen before. Murrell said nothing; he sat braced in his saddle, as a man not yet sure of himself, staring at the road in front. Perhaps his fever had left him too weak to talk much and he chose to remain silent, perhaps he was thinking some new and strange thoughts that had never

* Robert M. Coates, **The Outlaw Years,** pp. 210 - 211.

struck him before. Whatever the thoughts were behind those dark, hard-set eyes that day, he chose to keep to himself, and rode silently on. Murrell never talked of the occurrence; but years later, at the height of his infamous career, a sudden notion gripped him and he rode straight across the country to Columbia to find the girl and marry her. She was dead.

Murrell rode back to Memphis. He took a girl from the red-light district of the Gut, instead.

Whatever her origin may have been, once she cast her lot with Murrell she stuck. Through all his troubles she stayed near him. And some believed that she was in the heart of his conspiracy. If such was true, it was never proven. Nor was it ever proven that she was even privy to his diabolical plot.

The western district of Tennessee was a wild sparsely settled country, a reckless, backwoods frontier wilderness. Neighbors did not meet often; the population changed rapidly; men lived hard, struggling desperately against the grim dangers of the dark forest with little thought beyond that of their own self-preservation and that of their families. People lived pretty much to themselves and asked few questions. Madison County seemed remote and safe to Murrell. It looked like a good place for negro-stealing.

The younger brother, William, lived in Tipton County. The arrangement was convenient for the two to work together running negroes. John, in his travels, had learned many tricks of the trade. He now felt that he knew all the angles.

Murrell knew how to appeal to the simple soul of the darkey. Once he gained the negro's confidence, the rest was easy.

An account of a conversation in which Murrell approached a slave on the matter of running away has been handed down by a companion who was with him that day. It ran somewhat as follows:

An old grey-headed negro was seen bending under the weight of a heavy sack of corn which he was carrying to mill.

"Well, old man, you must have a hard master, or he would not send you to mill this cold day," Murrell accosted the old darkey.

"Yes, Massa, all ub um hard in dis country."

"Why do you stay with the villain, then, when he treats you like a dog?"

"I can't help um, Massa,"

"Would you help it if you could?"

"Oh! Yessah, Massa, dat I would."

"What is your name, old man?"

"My name Clitto, Massa."

"Well, Clitto, would you like to be free, and have plenty of money to buy lands, and horses, and everything you want?"

"Oh! Yes, Massa. Clitto sho' would."

"If I will steal you, carry you off, and sell you four or five times, give you half the money, and then leave you in a free state, will you go?"

"Oh! Yes, Massa, Clitto go quick."

"Well, Clitto, don't you want a dram this cold morning?"

Murrell produced a flask of liquor from his pocket and offered it to the darkey.

The old slave was startled at such etiquette. He declined in his best Southern manner. But the good man insisted.

"Only after you, Clitto," Murrell coaxed.

Clitto drank and then returned the flask to Murrell. Then Murrell turned the flask up and took a drink.

"Clitto, have you no boys you would like to see free?"

"Oh, yes, Massa."

"Now, Clitto, if you hear a pistol shot at the head of the lane some night, do you think you will be sure to come to me and bring three or four boys with you?"

"Oh, Yes, Massa, Clitto come dis very night."

"I am in a hurry now, Clitto, and can't carry you off at this time; but you must have the boys in readiness, and you shall not be with your task-master much longer to be cuffed and abused like a dog. I am a great friend to the black people. I have carried off a great many, and they are doing well; have homes of their own, and are making money. You must keep a bright look-out now, and when you hear the pistol fire, come with the boys. I will have horses ready to take you away. Farewell, Clitto, until I see you again."

The old darkey was left, bright with smiles.

"Fifteen minutes are all that I require to decoy the best of negroes from the best of masters," Murrell commented.

John constantly emphasized to William, with pride, that slave stealing in the backwoods country was a cinch for a smart man.

After a while William moved into Madison County. John needed him closer. Business was good.

If the people of Madison County became suspicious of Murrell's long absences from home, they were slow to voice an opinion. No one was anxious to make an accusation against Murrell. With all his "genteel manners" there was something about the man to make people fear him. He was not a character to be intimidated, and he let his neighbors know it. Once his wrath was aroused he made exceptions of no one. "They may now look out for breakers. Their long prayers and Methodist coats shall be no protection against my sworn vengeance; neither will they ever see their negroes if once they shall fall into my hands."

Murrell well knew how to defend himself when trouble came. He once spoke of himself and younger brother in the third person: "There are two young men who moved down from middle Tennessee to Madison County, keen, shrewd fellows; the eldest brother is one of the best judges of law in the United States. He directs the operations of the banditti; and he paves the way to all his offences that the law cannot reach him."

But he became so active and confident of himself that he grew bold as well as careless. He was caught redhanded.

The case exemplified his shrewdness and judgment in dealing with the law. It showed that his bragging was not entirely vain boasting.

Three negroes belonging to a certain Mr. Long of Madison County were decoyed from the owner's possession and harbored in a dense wood near his house. Everything worked off according to plan until the day before the negroes were to be removed to another section of the country. On that day one of the negroes left the group and ventured back to the plantation for some clothing which he had left. The overseer happened to see him, captured him, and extorted from him the location of his fellow servants. The designs of Murrell leaked out. A company of guards was immediately formed, and, under the leadership of Mr. Long, they marched into the woods and surrounded the negroes. The captured servant was used as a pilot. From the negroes Mr. Long found out what time Murrell would come to feed them. Then he instructed his slaves to ask

Murrell certain questions concerning his moving them. Members of the company were stationed in hiding around them in the undergrowth so as to hear Murrell's answers to the questions of the slaves.

True to the negro's statement, Murrell appeared at the designated time with a basket on his arm. The questions were asked while the men listened breathlessly in the bushes. It was a tense moment, for no one could know what trick this dangerous man might pull.

After hearing the answers, Long gave the signal for Murrell to be seized. The guards rushed from their hiding places in a vicious, triumphant dash with guns drawn. But to the surprise of all, there was no excitement. Murrell was calm and made not the least show of resistance. He looked at the men as if they had all made asses of themselves. He assumed his best manner and with quite dignity informed Mr. Long in a most business-like tone that he had found his slaves, and had been feeding them there so as to detain them until he could inform the owner where they were.

Mr. Long was not impressed, and the accused negro-stealer was promptly lodged in prison. But a surprising thing happened. It was only a few hours before Long and his friends saw Murrell riding about the country again as free as a bird. Many friends of the accused had appeared to offer bail for him.

In many conversations with his neighbors he told how Long, because of an old grudge, had framed him and was persecuting him. Many people believed his story. He seemed so sincere and hurt about it.

When the day of the trial came the courthouse was thronged. Many thought he was good for the penitentiary. The defendant played a bold part. He laughed in court about the matter. His charge was only a finable offence, at most, he said. The court was a bunch of fools; and they could make the worst of it and be damned! He had employed a lawyer by the name of Andrew L. Martin for his attorney. The attorney was a "flowery fellow." The offender wanted a man who was convincing and who could talk well. The amount of law that he knew was not important. Murrell would attend to that himself. He wanted a man who could follow instructions.

After the trial got under way Murrell decided that Martin was getting nowhere. During the evidence the defendant took the attorney aside, cursed him, and emphasized that he was being paid to work according to instructions. The attorney wanted to direct the case himself. But he was losing. Murrell firmly informed his counsel that if he did not work as he was told, he would kick him out of the courtroom. Martin was elegant enough, but "he had not dived into the quirks of the law like his client."

As it turned out, Murrell was not imprisoned; but he was fined and ordered by the court to pay the cost of the suit. In case his property would not cover the cost, he was to become Long's slave for five years. Murrell immediately questioned the constitutionality of such a procedure. He was not alarmed, merely amused. He referred to the judge as "an old fool of a squire, who neither knew nor cared for the law or his duty, and would have committed him against positive proof." When the verdict was read out in court, he winked at Long and called him Master Billy.

But Murrell did not intend ever to pay the fine and cost. After the trial he disposed of Martin's services after telling him he was "not worth a damn." He took matters into his own hands. He told the court that the case had not been conducted according to legal procedure and, to carry his point, cited laws and decisions. He tangled the

opposing attorneys and the judge; he made the courtroom
roar with laughter until many people considered the whole
matter a joke. When the judge failed to drop the case,
it was appealed to the higher court. But when that step
was gained, Murrell picked a technical flaw, and the case
never came to trial again.

Doubtless Murrell did not have the legal right to
handle his own case in such a manner, but apparently he
had the officials too confused to know just how to stop
him.

Long and his friends were indignant as well as em-
barassed. It was clear that Murrell had outwitted them.
Many considered the joke on Long. Believing that they
could do nothing with him at law, a group formed a company which they called Captain Slick's Company, and advertised for all honest men to meet at a certain school
house to bind themselves against him.

Careful plans were laid. Rules and laws for the government of the company were made. Murrell was declared
a menace to society. He must be done away with, and no
pains were spared in preparing to do it. They would deal
with him this time in a way where his smart law tricks
could do him no good.

On a certain night, which had been announced, the
company of over two dozen men came marching up to
Murrell's house, with their guns flashing. It was to be
the last of the slick negro-stealer.

But Murrell had read the notices of Slick's Company,
and he had friends the same as Long. Eighteen were with
him on that night. And they were well supplied with guns
and ammunition. The dwelling and outbuildings had been
prepared with portholes, and men were stationed about
in them, organized as if under some skilled general's orders.
Men were stationed in different buildings so as to command a fair fire to rake the door of the dwelling.

And so Long and his men came creeping on in the silence of the night with no voice to warn them of what lay ahead. But before reaching the house, they discovered the musket barrels pointing out at them from the building with deadly aim. They stood frozen in their tracks for a moment. Their aggressive rage turned suddenly into tremulous fear. They were afraid to huddle together for a conference. Any move might be fatal. Without any command to retreat, they turned and made as inconspicuous an exit as possible. They decided that the safest thing to do was to let Murrell alone. Murrell had told his friends around him that the law would uphold a man in the protection of his home. Perhaps it would. Doutbless Murrell knew.

It has been said that Murrell was never known to show mercy to anyone who happened to come within his power or to anyone at whom he was angered. To his last days he was a devout believer in the aphorism that dead men tell no tales. But after he moved down into Madison County an incident occurred which proved an exception. It is the only record of the blood-thirsty bandit ever having shown mercy to one who became helpless before him:

It was in the summer of 1832, so the story goes. Three dust-covered men astride sweaty horses pulled reins abruptly in front of a large plantation home in west Tennessee. A lady appeared at the door of the big house. And immediately the leader of the party demanded food for his men.

"I should be glad to have you served, gentlemen," was the hospitable response. "Won't you come in and rest meanwhile?"

But the leader, who was Murrell in one of his worst moods, replied gruffly that they preferred waiting beside their horses while preparations were being made. He emphasized that he was in a hurry.

The lady of the house was Mrs. Blanchard, wife of Colonel Archer Blanchard, a wealthy planter. At the time, Colonel Blanchard was at Nashville attending to business.

When Mrs. Blanchard went to her kitchen she found that the cook had gone to the negro quarters, a few hundred yards away. To recall her she took down the big hunting horn that hung at the end of the porch, and placing it to her lips gave a sonorous blast upon it. But the summons was never completed. A pistol cracked, and the horn went spinning from her hands and fell clattering to the porch floor. The startled lady turned quickly in the direction of her uninvited guests. One of the men was making toward her, while the leader coolly lowered his pistol and replaced it in its holster.

"What are you trying to do?" he yelled at the woman, as his companions seized the excited hostess by the wrist. "Who are you calling, woman?"

"I was calling the cook who had gone to the quarters," she explained indignantly, wrenching her hand free. "I was trying to serve you, but it seems to me," and she drew herself up undauntedly and flashed defiance at them all, "that you had better ride on your way now. There are others about the plantation who are not so defenseless as I seem."

"By God, she's right, John," cried the man who had released the woman. "The sooner we get away the better."

The advice was taken and the men returned to their horses. They were in the act of mounting when one of the animals bit viciously at another; and the attacked horse lashed out with both feet.

Murrell was standing with his back toward the kicking horse and directly in the way of its flying feet. The animal's feet pounded into the side of his body, and with a sharp groan he staggered and fell beside the yard fence.

His comrades rushed to him, but he was limp and unconscious.

Mrs. Blanchard fluttered down from the porch and unceremoniously took charge. "He's badly hurt. Bring him into the house," she directed, and they obeyed without question or comment.

Restoratives were promptly applied and soon the injured man was conscious once more; but when he attempted to sit up on the couch where he had been placed, he fell back with a loud groan.

His comrades stood by, stiff with bewilderment at this sudden turn of events. They did not know what to do. But after a while Murrell recovered sufficiently to talk.

"I'm hurt too badly to go on," he announced crisply. "I've got to stay here and take my chances. You two leave at once, and ride as far as you can tonight. Push on to Stockworth's by tomorrow. At least, go."

It was some time after the men disappeared that Murrell spoke again. He addressed his hostess:

"I'm at your mercy, madam," he said tersely. "You owe me no good will and—"

"You are a human creature, and you are hurt," Mrs. Blanchard said simply. "You have the claims upon me that every such creature has. I can think of nothing else while you need aid."

"You are generous, madam, you are generous," was the grim answer. "At any rate, I am in your hands."

For two days the injured outlaw lay at the Blanchard home and received the ministrations of its mistress. Mrs. Blanchard was attentive, but Murrell was annoyed by the friendly advances of little Archer junior. The child wanted to show him everything about the house. More

than once the youngster insisted upon having the strange
guest admire the cherished miniature painting of his
father, one of the family treasures which the boy brought
to him with the childish prattle of "daddy." Murrell only
grunted. On the morning of the third day he took a shame-
ful departure.

It was several days later before Mrs. Blanchard was
informed of the identity of the man she had nursed. When
reprimanded for her act, she said simply: "He was hurt,
and he was my guest; I couldn't have done otherwise."

In the fall of 1833 Colonel Blanchard was again on
his way to Nashville to attend to business interests. He
had traveled about half the distance between Jackson and
Nashville, when he was suddenly confronted in the road
by two masked men, who presented pistols and ordered
him to stand and deliver. Instead of obeying, Colonel
Blanchard attempted to draw his own weapon to defend
himself.

But the bandits were too quick for him. Both fired
at him the same moment. One of them missed, the bullet
burying in the saddle. The other bullet struck him a
glancing blow on the side of the head. He came tumbling
senselessly to the ground.

The highwaymen immediately relieved his person of
several thousand dollars, his watch, and diamond ring.
When he regained consciousness he was lying tied in the
shade of a big sycamore tree some distance within the
forest.

He concealed the fact that he was conscious. He
listened to the men.

"Slit his throat," he heard one of them say. "Then
we'll gut him and sink him in the creek."

Preparations for the operation were under way when
a tall man suddenly stepped out from the underbrush. He

demanded what had happened. It was clear that he was
the leader of the party. He was told what had taken place
and how much had been found on him. The figure delighted Murrell.

"But what has been done about the prisoner?" he asked
thoughtfully.

"He's stunned; that's all," was the answer.

"We can't have that," Murrell announced sharply.
"Take him to the creek and attend to his case there. You
know what to do."

But as the highwaymen passed Murrell, he suddenly
threw up his hands and ordered the procession to stop. He
stepped hastily over to take a closer view of the prisoner.
Then he astonished the gang by ordering them to release
the prisoner at once. This was strange! The men de-
murred, but orders from Murrell were not to be questioned.
Grumblingly they obeyed.

Murrell ordered Blanchard's belongings returned to
him. He instructed the man how to get back to the road
and on his way again.

Colonel Blanchard raised his voice to thank the outlaw, but Murrell sternly cut him short:

"You owe me nothing," he said. "I am not returning
your goods and sparing your life because I have taken a
liking to you, or because I am afraid to carry out the
wishes of my men. I am paying a debt that I owe your
wife. Mrs. Blanchard can tell you why you were spared . . .
if she has not already done so."

The colonel could not resist a parting question: "I
have never seen you, Sir," he asserted, "and I do not think
that you have ever seen me. Will you tell me how you
recognized me?"

For a moment the outlaw's grim features relaxed into
the semblance of a smile and he answered more civilly.

"It is true that I have not the honor of Colonel Blanchard's acquaintance, but I have seen his wife and son; and the boy has shown me his picture. The likeness was a good one. And now, Sir, if you regard your good health, lose no time in getting on your way."

And it is also recorded that the colonel took the advice.

Murrell was a hard man for the backwoodsmen to understand. Bad rumors circulated about him, part of them so inhuman and fantastic that some discredited them all. People who had definite ideas about the man tactfully kept them to themselves.

A Tennessee historian gave the following description of Murrell, and such must have been about the kind of citizen many of the inhabitants of Madison County knew: "He possessed a quick mind and a remarkably pleasant and gentleman-like address. He had great natural adaptability and was as much at ease among people of refinement as among his clansmen. He had a certain frank, cordial manner that enabled him at times to convert his bitterest enemies into his warmest admirers. . . . He had a cool, clear-headed judgment, and was utterly without fear, physical or moral. His ascendency over men never waned. And they were ever ready to sacrifice their lives in order to save his. Within the ranks of his clan he was just, fair and amiable. He was a kind husband and brother, and a faithful friend."

But there was one weak spot in his armor. It was his conceit. Murrell had a nefarious ambition that took pride in his position and in the operation of his followers, independent of the love of gain. He was vain and eager to lead. The man had a vain desire to impress people with his importance. This made for too much talk, and it led to his downfall.

Chapter XI.

AN AMATEUR DETECTIVE

IN the late afternoon of January 21, 1834, a handsome young man by the name of Virgil A. Stewart pulled reins in front of the home of the Reverend John Henning in Madison County, Tennessee. He had reached the end of a three days' journey from the Choctaw Purchase. He found a warm welcome. He was a good friend of the family and at one time had been a neighbor. They were glad that he had come to pay them a visit.

But Stewart soon saw below the pleasantries of his welcome a gloom that he had never before seen in this house. It made him a bit uncomfortable. Could it be caused by his appearance; and was his welcome a forced courtesy?

At the supper table there was talk of old times and of affairs in the Purchase. How was Stewart doing there? Was business good? Had he bought land? Were the Indians peaceful? For a time the visitor forgot his unpleasant observations. He talked freely of his six months stay in the Choctaw Purchase.

It was long after Mrs. Henning had cleared the supper dishes away before Stewart found out the cause of the gloom that hung over the household. Someone was stealing the Reverend Henning's negroes. The old minister was none too well fixed and the loss of a slave was a serious matter. He was greatly distressed.

On the night of the 18th two of his best negro men had disappeared. The old preacher did not want to accuse anyone unjustly. But finally it came out that a certain John A. Murrell, a neighbor, was looked upon with suspicion. His long absences from home had been a topic of conversation in the neighborhood.

Murrell had become a sort of backwoods dandy. His suits were of the latest cuts, his hats of the nicest silk with "a rim three-quarters inches wide," his boots of the choicest calf skin. He flashed this make-up before his neighbors. It was becoming noticeable to a few. He carried his head high; there was something in his face that gave the Reverend Henning an uncomfortable feeling. The backwoods minister was not impressed with this air of finery. He wanted to call the man a rascal. But being a God-fearing man, he hesitated.

Mrs. Henning was not so reserved. She believed that this slick dandy was a thief and a scoundrel. And she told Stewart so. "He's a big hypocrite," she said; and produced a letter to prove her point.

She handed Stewart a folded letter. It was a neatly written thing, with a handwriting that might have been the envy of the frontier. It was addressed to the Reverend Henning and signed by John A. Murrell. It had come to Murrell's attention that it was being rumored in the community that he had stolen the old preacher's negroes. The letter proved Murrell a master at making phrases. It was a bit too flowery. But at that it was well done. He wrote of "his long and earnestly continued friendship." He was hurt that any neighbor should so unjustly accuse him. He insisted that his activities were "clear and open as the day." He wrote that he would be glad to see the Reverend Henning, but he had to leave on a business trip to Randolph, a town a short distance above Memphis, on the 25th of January. But as soon as he should return he would welcome a full investigation.

The family was not impressed with Murrell's nice phrases. Reverend Henning wished that something might be done to get his slaves back. But he knew little to suggest.

Before the night was passed a plan was agreed upon. Stewart offered his assistance in helping in any possible way to bring back the old parson's slaves. It was planned that when Murrell rode out on his trip the 25th, Stewart and the parson's son, Richard, would follow Murrell. For it was believed that Murrell would go to the place where the negroes were hidden just as soon as the excitement of the theft had subsided. Just how the young men would handle the situation was not settled. But young Stewart thrilled over the prospective detective adventure, the prospects of recovering his old friend's slaves.

Virgil Stewart was an adventurer by nature. Circumstance had always kept him moving. He was born in the state of Georgia, the son of well-to-do parents. When he was yet an infant, his father, Samuel Stewart, migrated to Amite County in Mississippi, where he died a few months after his arrival. Mrs. Stewart did not like Mississippi, and soon returned to Georgia. And it was here that Virgil grew up to manhood. At the age of fourteen he left school to go to work. Most of the family fortune had been squandered, so Virgil's hope for a classical education was abandoned.

After leaving school he engaged in the printing business, an employment he thought best suited to improve his mind. This failed to hold his attention, and he next went into a co-partnership manufacturing cotton gins, an enterprise that turned out rather profitably.

By the time he was twenty he had dissolved partnership in the gin manufacturing business and set out for the West. He arrived in Madison County in the fall of 1830 with several slaves and settled on a farm six miles from Jackson. The Hennings had been very kind neighbors. Parson Henning had helped the young man establish himself. He had even advanced a small loan to help in paying for the farm.

Then hearing of rich lands being opened up in the Choctaw Purchase, Stewart decided to sell his property and remove to the Purchase and invest all his capital in land in that country.

Parson Henning had expressed regret in seeing him leave. He had learned to like the young man, for he was industrious and intelligent, and highly respected by those who knew him. But the lure of the new lands being opened up was too much for young Stewart. He sold his property and with part of the proceeds purchased merchandise which he expected to sell with profit to the Indians and early settlers of that region.

On the first day of June, 1833, Stewart left Jackson, bound for Tuscahoma in the Choctaw Purchase. About a mile north of Tuscahoma he had a house built for the reception of his goods.

In the Purchase, he had first lived with a Mr. Edward Clanton, a store-keeper in Tuscahoma. While waiting for the land sales, Stewart had found much time on his hands. Clanton was away from home a considerable part of his time. He asked Stewart to attend to his store during his absences, and in return he gave him his board and lodging. A bargain was struck, because Stewart was as yet occupied

but little with his own business. About two weeks before
Stewart left the Purchase, Clanton had returned after an
absence of some weeks with his family. There was not
room in Clanton's cabin now for Stewart. So Clanton
recommended the Vess family who lived nearby. Stewart
did not like his new home so well. Whereas Clanton was
a rather well-to-do man, William Vess appeared a shiftless sort who stayed away from home most of the time.
He gave his occupation as that of a journeyman carpenter.
It was natural that one of this trade might be away from
home a great deal. Stewart never questioned his absences.
The couple was friendly, and Mrs. Vess was very kind and
an excellent cook. He had stayed on.

On the morning of January 26, 1934, Virgil Stewart
was at Denmark, Tennessee, waiting for Richard Henning.
Stewart had ridden on ahead to Denmark during the night
of the 25th. He wanted to travel at night in order not to
be seen. Richard had promised to join him there. Stewart
remained in Denmark several hours, waiting for young
Henning, but his intended companion never came; and
finally, fearing that a further delay might cause them to
miss Murrell, Stewart rode alone toward the settlement of
Estanaula. He supposed that Richard Henning had taken
ill.

Just why the date of Murrell's departure turned out
to be the 26th instead of the 25th the records do not show.
But the 26th of January, 1834, turned out to be a tragic
date in Murrell's life. It marked the turning point in his
career.

The morning was cold and sleety; the road was frozen,
and travel was difficult. Stewart poked on hoping that
Murrell might overtake him. When he reached the toll
bridge across the Big Hatchee River at Estanaula he in-

quired of the keeper if he knew a man named Murrell from up near Jackson. Yes, the bridge tender knew him. "Has he passed this way this morning?" Stewart asked. The gateman had seen nothing of him; but Murrell often passed that way. "Well, if he passes this morning, I want you to point him out to me, but don't let him know about it."

Stewart waited. Several horsemen came splashing along the sleet covered trace. They would rein up at the toll house, pay their fees, and push their mounts on Westward again. After each traveler had passed Stewart would question the keeper. No, Murrell had not passed. He would let him know.

Finally, almost before anyone saw him a distinguishedly dressed man reined up at the toll gate, paid his fare and was off again in a trot. The men marvelled at the fine horse the man rode.

"That's Murrell," the keeper said when the handsome rider had passed. "Nobody could mistake Murrell; he's the best dressed man in these parts."

Stewart thanked the keeper, paid his toll and followed on across the bridge.

After a short while Stewart gave his horse a free rein and overtook Murrell. The men exchanged greetings.

"We have disagreeable weather for traveling,"* Stewart began simply.

"Extremely so, sir," the well dressed man replied.

"The travelling and my business correspond well," Stewart continued.

"What can be your business that you should compare it to traveling on such a road as this?"

---

* The dialogues between Stewart and Murrell are taken from Stewart's account of the detection. Stewart secretly took notes during the trip and shortly afterwards wrote a lengthy account of the whole affair.

"Horse-hunting, sir."

"Yes, yes, disagreeable indeed. Your comparison is not a bad one. Where did your horse stray from?"

"From Yallabusha River in the Choctaw Purchase."

"Where is he aiming for?"

"I do not know; I am told he was owned by a man in this country somewhere; but it is an uncertain business— a cross-and-pile chance."

"How far will you go?"

"I don't know. The roads are so very bad, and the weather so extremely cold, I am becoming very tired of so uncertain a business; and I am quite lonesome traveling by myself. How far down will you go on this road?"

"About eighteen miles, to the house of a friend. I am anxious to get there tonight, but it will be very late traveling in such cold weather. Perhaps your horse is stolen."

"No, I guess not, though I had rather some clever fellow had stolen him than that he should be straying."

At that, Murrell's countenance brightened into a delicate, amused grin; he straightened a bit in his saddle as if stimulated to give a speech. But in a moment all signs of interest were gone as quickly as they had appeared. The man was again the hardened bandit hidden behind a rich garb and reserved face.

"Yes, quite a bit of robbing and stealing going on in this country," Murrell answered casually.

The men rode on silently. Stewart's hope fell. He dared not say more at the time. Only the splashing of the horses' hoofs in the half-melted sleet broke the crisp silence of the wilderness.

Then it was Murrell who broke the silence. Perhaps he had been thinking. "Are you acquainted in this part of the country?"

"I am a stranger, sir."

"Where are you from?"

"I was born in the state of Georgia, and brought up here; but have moved to the Choctaw Purchase, and have been there about nine or ten months."

"How do you like that country?"

"Very well, indeed."

Murrell's interest in the country came out in his next question:

"Is there much stealing going on in that country?"

"No, not much, considering we are pretty much savages and forerunners. You know how all new countries are generally first settled."

"Certainly. I am well acquainted with these things."

It must have eased Murrell's feelings a bit to hear that his companion was from Georgia and had resided in the Choctaw Purchase for only nine or ten months. The man could know nothing of him! The cool morning air was stimulating. Murrell wanted to talk.

It was not unnatural that his conversation should drift to the subject of stealing and the wild country of the frontier:

"This country is about to be completely overrun by a company of rogues; and they are so strong that nothing can be done with them. They steal from whom they please; and if the person they take from accuses them, they jump on more of his property. And it is found that it is best to be friendly with them. They are two young men who moved down from middle Tennessee to Madison County, keen, shrewd, fellows, they are." He told what a smart judge of law the oldest brother was and how he directed the operations of the banditti; and so paved the way to all their offences that the law could not reach them.

Murrell was engaging in his narrative. He had an oily tongue, and being the vain creature that he was, he loved to use it and to know that others marveled at his gift.

And Stewart, the young detective, listened. His gasps and gestures made it clear that he was much interested. He admired such shrewd fellows as his companion described, so he led Murrell to believe. He replied:

"Well, sir, if they have sense enough to evade the laws of their country, which are made by the wisest men of the nation, let them do it. It is just as honorable for them to gain property by their superior powers as it is for a long-faced hypocrite to take advantage of the necessities of his fellow-beings."

Stewart paused for a moment to observe Murrell's reaction. The outlaw was interested. Stewart continued with his speech: "We are placed here, and we must act for ourselves. . . . What is it that constitutes character, popularity, and power, in the United States? Sir, it is property; strip a man of his property in this country, and he is a ruined man indeed—you see his friends forsake him, and he may have been raised in the highest circles of society, yet he is neglected and treated with contempt. Sir, my doctrine is, let the hardest fend off."

"You have expressed my sentiments and feelings better than I could myself; and I am happy to fall in company possessed of principles so congenial with my own. I have no doubt these two brothers are as honorable among their associates and clan as any men on earth, but perfect devils to their enemies."

And so the slick-tongued Murrell rambled on. The men were riding through a wild, rough country where outlaws and clever exploits were the talk of the day. There were certain stories current of these shrewd brothers that the backswoodsmen were forever telling. He would feed his vanity by telling of some of their clever exploits, in the third person, of course, and watch this admiring chap marvel.

Murrell told of the Long case, how the law had tried to get the elder brother for taking the slaves of a certain Mr. Long, and then how a mob tried to take him after the law failed. It had not been so long since, and Murrell enjoyed telling the details. "It's the law that settles all these matters," Murrell explained. "Let a man learn the use of the law and nothing can touch him." He told how Murrell had kicked his lawyer out of the court room, pleaded his own case and won.

And Stewart all gapes and stares asked how a man might do such remarkable things.

"He is a fellow of such smooth and genteel manners that he is very imposing, and many of the more credulous part of the community are induced to believe that he was persecuted by Long, when he intended only friendship and kindness in catching his negroes for him. He well knows how to excite the sympathy of the human heart, and turn things to his advantage. He rarely fails to captivate the feelings of those whom he undertakes; and, what is more astonishing, he succeeds in many instances where the strongest prejudice has existed; and, where his revenge has been excited, he never fails to effect either the destruction of their property or character, and frequently both. . .

"There is an old Methodist preacher and his son who had two very fine negro men stolen a short time back, and this old Parson Henning and his son were officious in procuring counsel, and expressing their sentiments about him and his brother, and saying what the country ought to do with them, and all such stuff as this. And I have no doubt but those two young men have got them." Murrell paused to smile, and then added:

"They live within about two miles of the old preacher,

and he and his son are as much afraid of those two young
men as if they were ravenous beasts and were turned
loose in the forest. If they were sure of finding their
negroes by following them off, they would sooner lose their
property than fall into the hands of those dreaded men."

This may explain why Richard Henning never showed
up at Denmark to accompany Stewart.

At sunset the men dropped into a beautiful dale known
as Popular Creek Valley. The late sun reflected a brilliant
red through the icy tops of the half-frozen poplars. The
men rode straight on into the sunset.

As night came on the air turned to a crisp, chilling
blast. The shadows of the poplars lengthened and cast
intricate, gruesome patterns on the ground before the
travelers. To Stewart, a nervous, apprehensive day turned
suddenly into a mysterious, dangerous night.

"We will spend the night at an old friend of mine,"
Murrell announced.

A chill went over Stewart. The home of Murrell's
friend might be a scene of his horrible crimes, perhaps a
hide-out for associates. Worse still, what if Parson Henning's negroes were there, and should recognize him? His
recognition would likely mean death. Murrell would
never let him get away while he lived, if he could prevent
it. He had talked too much. But it was too late to turn
back now. Stewart followed on.

A burning log was discovered near the roadside.
Murrell suggested that they stop and warm. It was too
dark for traveling anyway. They would have to wait for
the moon to rise. Stewart climbed down from his horse
awkwardly. He had some difficulty in walking from his
horse to the fire. He was frozen almost stiff.

"You appear very cold, my young friend," said Murrell as they seated themselves by the fire; "I fear you are frosted; you can't stand it like me—I have undergone enough to kill a horse."

After about half an hour the moon rose in a clear cold sky. The men mounted and set out for the friend's house. It was better traveling now. But Stewart lagged behind. At the thought of entering this strange, unknown home, a wave of fear gripped him. He had only one single-shot pistol. If Murrell should prove faithless in the midst of his friends he felt himself unequal to a contest. He held back on his bridle reins. If the treacherous Murrell should suddenly turn suspicious Stewart wanted the advantage of being in the rear. He kept his hand on his pistol.

But Murrell insisted that Stewart ride up. "Come, sir, the night is cold and we have far to go. Let us pass the time as pleasantly as possible. Ride up and I will tell you of another feat of this elder brother of whom I have been speaking."

Murrell turned again to the same gloomy topics of robbery and murder. He told how the handsome, well-dressed elder brother often deceived the people by "dressing in the Methodist order. . . . He preaches a hell of a fine sermon." He gave clever examples of his preaching, how he stole negroes and passed out counterfeit money among the brethren. It was all very amusing; and Murrell seemed to forget the cold as he talked.

And Stewart laughed heartily at the funny things this marvelous man did. Murrell rattled on, engrossed with his own vain sayings, until the cabin of the friend appeared in a small clearing.

"Well, sir, we are nearing my old friend's place. Will

you go as far down as Randolph? Your horse may have got down in that region."

Stewart said that he did not know. He wanted to go on until he could find his horse, but he was scarce of change. Stewart wanted an excuse for turning back. If he found Henning's negroes at the friend's house his journey would probably end there. And then, on the other hand, he did not want to appear a good prospect for robbing. He had no assurance that Murrell was not setting a trap for him.

"I'm going to Arkansas, and I would be glad if you would go over with me. I'll let you have money if you get out; and I'll show you the country. I have thousands of friends there; it will not cost us a cent if we stay six months. And I'll carry you where you can bring away a better horse than the one you are hunting. I'll learn you a few tricks if you will go with me. A man with as keen an eye as yours should never spend his time hunting a horse."

Stewart thanked him. He would determine tomorrow whether or not he would go.

The midnight visitors knocked for admittance at the country cabin. A moment, and the door was opened. They walked in and were received with much attention and respect. Stewart's eyes glanced hastily around the apartment in search of the old parson's slaves. They were not in sight.

Stewart was weary from his long, cold ride. It had been a straining day. After sitting for a short time before the fire he called for lodgings and left Murrell and his friends engaged in conversation before the fire.

Alone in his room he hastily scribbled the events of the day in his blank notebook. Then he slipped into bed.

But the terrible thoughts of what the morning might bring kept him awake for hours. What if the Henning negroes should recognize him before he had an opportunity to appraise them of the situation?

It was terrible to think what might happen. It was near morning before Stewart slept.

CHAPTER XII

MURRELL REVEALS HIS PLANS

STEWART was up early next morning. He had slept but little. He wanted to take advantage of the early hour to stroll over the premises in search of Parson Henning's negroes; intending in the event of finding them to appraise them of his purpose and instruct them not to recognize him in the presence of Murrell. But he could find nothing of them. And upon satisfying himself that they were not there, he returned to the house where he found Murrell prepared to ride, and giving directions for their horses.

Stewart had been careful to make particular inquiry of his stray horse in Murrell's presence.

The men were on the road at an early hour. They had not ridden far when Murrell inquired for the first time the name of his companion. In that country strangers asked few questions. It was a practice of the day.

"I seldom ever have a name; though you may call me Hues at present—Adam Hues," Stewart responded.

"Well, Mr. Hues, what say you of the trip to Arkansas this morning?"

"I have not yet fairly determined on that matter; though I think I will go."

There was little for Stewart to decide. Whether he wanted to go or turn back, he felt now, was not a matter entirely in his hands. He feared to decline Murrell's invitation. Murrell had told him too much.

"Go; yes, you must go, and I will make a man of you."

"That is what I want, sir."

"There are some of the handsomest girls over there you ever saw. I am in town when I am there."

"Nothing to object to, sir; I am quite partial to handsome ladies."

"Oh! Well, go with me to Arkansas, and damn me if I don't put you right in town, and they are as plump as ever came over, sir."

"I think I will go, sir. I will determine down about Wesley."

"We can strike a breeze worth telling over there," Murrell insisted.

"I do not doubt it, sir."

The men went jogging on until most of the morning had passed. Then a serious problem arose for Stewart. They were nearing the town of Wesley, and Stewart had three good friends there who might recognize him in the presence of Murrell. If they should divulge his proper name and perchance inquire of friends in Madison County, serious consequences would result. Stewart was startled. He had been so busy listening to Murrell's exploits that he had neglected laying any definite plans.

They were entering the town. "We'll have a warm here," Murrell suggested.

Stewart knew it was coming. They would have to

stop. Surely they needed to warm. And then it was almost time for dinner.

"Yes, sir, we will have something to eat at the tavern," Stewart responded boldly, "and buy some brandy."

"We will get the brandy, but I have lots of provisions in my portmanteau," Murrell informed him.

The thought of the brandy turned out to be an idea. It also occurred to Stewart that his character of horse-hunter might be of use in furnishing an excuse to separate for a short time from Murrell. If he could just get away a few minutes he might be able to contact his friends and let them know the nature of his business. So at the edge of the village Stewart drew forth a flask and asked Murrell if he would have it filled, while he would stop at the first store and write some advertisements for his stray horse. They would save time this way. The outlaw assented agreeably, and rode off toward the Wesley Inn.

Stewart remained at the first store on the edge of town until he saw Murrell enter the tavern. As soon as Murrell disappeared he made his way to a grocery kept by one of his friends, with a view of putting him on his guard. The friend was out of town. Good enough!

Another friend lived at the tavern. And Stewart knew that Murrell would soon be leaving there because another of his acquaintances owned the only store where retail liquor was sold.

In a few minutes he saw Murrell leave the tavern with his flask in search of liquor. Stewart ducked away, and as soon as Murrell was out of sight set out quickly for the tavern. There he soon found his friend, Colonel Bayliss, sitting in the tavern. He told him hastily of his designs so that he might pass him off as a stranger. Colonel Bayliss loaned him a pistol. He tucked it carefully away and felt safer.

When Murrell returned to the tavern he found his companion, Hues, seated comfortably before the fire warming himself. Colonel Bayliss, a most unconcerned stranger, sat nearby.

Hues intimated that he had expected to find him here after he had advertised for his horse.

"Couldn't get the damn stuff here," Murrell explained with some contempt.

They had a good drink together and both felt better.

They reined their horses toward Randolph. Murrell seemed eager to travel. About a mile out of town at a bend in the road Murrell pulled his horse from the road and spurred him sharply into the woods. He motioned for Stewart to follow. Stewart felt himself suddenly turn cold. What could the man mean? From such a man, he had come to expect anything. Yet he dared not turn back. He felt for his pistols to see that they were handy. He had the satisfaction of being in the rear, and he stayed there. Nervously he followed on, fearing what the next minute might bring.

Murrell led on until they came into a clearing well hidden from the road. Apparently Murrell knew where he was going. "We'll have a bite of cold victuals," Murrell announced bluntly, and commenced to dismount.

Stewart took a free breath. He might have thought of this before.

Murrell opened his saddle bag. There was jerked beef and bread, plenty of it; and the two men sat on a log eating until they had their fill. They washed the dry, cold food down with the brandy. Murrell felt talkative after the meal. He was again in his boastful mood.

"You have decided to go to Arkansas with me?" Murrell started.

Stewart answered that he had.

"Well, Hues, I think that I can put you in better business than trading with the Indians."

"I have no doubt of that, sir."

Murrell was silent for a moment. Then a peculiar smile spread over his face, a sort of self-conscious grin. "Did you ever hear of those devils, the Murrells, up in Madison County in this state?" he asked. He was looking at Stewart out of the corner of his eye.

Stewart started. He anticipated what was coming. In the most unconcerned manner he could summon, he replied: "I am an entire stranger to them, sir."

"Well, Hues," said Murrell, "I might as well be out with it. I am that older brother I have been telling you of!"

The two travelers went riding on toward Randolph. Now that Murrell had revealed himself he seemed to want to tell everything. "Sir, I am the leader of a noble band of valiant and lordly bandits; I will give you our plans and strength hereafter, and will introduce you among my fellows."

Stewart was amazed. "What next!" he wondered. He had suspected Murrell only as a notorious negro stealer. He did not know that the man headed an outlaw band. But perhaps the man was boasting. It was hard to believe that all Murrell had said could be true. But he would see. He would have to see now!

"Hues, I had not been in company with you more than two hours before I knew you as well as if I had made you, and could have trusted my life in your hands. A little practice is all that you want, and you can look into the very heart and thoughts of a man. The art of learning men is nothing when you once see how it is managed."

"Your confidence is a splendid compliment," Hues returned courteously.

"I will give you the names and residences of my friends before we part," Murrell continued. "But we must not be parted longer than you can arrange your business; and I'll make you a splendid fellow and put you on the high road to fortune."

Murrell was overwhelming with his confidence in Hues. Hues played his part, and let on that he considered his companion a great man. Murrell swallowed the bait, and hooked himself in the process.

"You shall be admitted to the grand council of our clan, for I consider you a young man of splendid abilities."

The grand council! Stewart wondered. He was to remember that. The mission was becoming mysterious.

Murrell looked up. He observed that the sun was getting low. He said that he would have to insist on his friend traveling all night. He had been delayed. "I am now going to the place whither I sent that old Methodist's negroes in charge of a friend. The time has already passed at which I promised to meet him. And I fear, being ignorant of the cause of my delay, he will become alarmed, and decline waiting for me."

Murrell explained how he had been delayed by the old parson up in Madison County. The old man had spied on him. He had even intended to follow him. "A keen conception of the old fellow's, and if he had known how to hold his tongue, and not been too anxious to let others know his thoughts, he might have given me some trouble; but I always have men to manage the case of such gentry as he and his son." He told of sending the letter. He explained to Stewart. "I can take Dick Henning by my side, and steal and make sale of every negro he and his father own, and receive the money for them, and he shall know nothing of the transaction."

"That would be a strange maneuver, sure!" Stewart gaped. "I should be pleased to learn how you would manage it."

"Simple enough," Murrell explained. "I would have an understanding with the negroes beforehand to meet me at a certain time and place. I would also employ a friend to meet them in my place and conduct them off to the morass whither we are now traveling. This arrangement made, I might be at home, or, if you please, at Henning's house, at the very time this friend was carrying off his negroes. I could then dispose of my interest in his negroes to *a friend*, and have my money counted out to me before his face, and he could know nothing of the transaction. True, I would not deliver the property, but my friend would know very well where to find it. It was never my intention, Hues, to disturb my immediate neighbors, until since they have commenced their sharp-shooting at me. They may now look out for the worst."

To satisfy his young pupil that he had not been guilty of misrepresentation in detailing his feats of villainy, he proposed to decoy the first negro they should meet on the road. They had not traveled far before the opportunity presented itself. They found an old negro man laboring near the roadside.

"Well, old man, you must have a hard master to make a man of your years labor so hard in this cold weather," Murrell began.

The old darkey, slow at first to complain of his master, after a few minutes opened up and was pouring out stories of hardships. Murrell offered him a drink of the brandy he had purchased at Wesley. He made the negro drink first. He had long since learned that this never failed to have its effect.

"Would you like to be free?" he asked the aged darkey, "and have all the good things that the white folks have?"

Before passing on the old negro had agreed with enthusiam to meet Murrell some night in the lane.

Hues was highly amused at the exhibition, and he expressed himself much pleased. He took occasion to compliment his success in achieving so speedy a conquest — he had learned the nearest way to Murrell's heart. Flattery. It had the desired effect. For Murrell turned to him with an air of self-complacency and triumph and said that what he had just done was but a trifling job.

As the darkness of the evening drew on Murrell talked of more important things than negro stealing. Heretofore he had talked only of petty robbery, negro running, clever tricks he had played on his neighbors, his shrewd deception as a Methodist preacher, occasionally of single handed murder. But now he talked of greater things, schemes horrible in their greatness. He no longer pictured himself as the lone outlaw. He would be a general, in his way, such as Andrew Jackson and Napoleon had been in theirs. He had talked as if for the pure vanity of it. Now he had become hard, and Stewart saw him turn from the clever, entertaining bandit to the terrible, bloodthirsty beast that he later knew him to be. Now that he knew Hues, he took him into his close confidence. He wanted to talk business. The man was not boasting now. The lines in his face hardened as only a bitter soul might draw them. "I look on the American people as my common enemy," he said. "They have disgraced me, and they can do no more. My life is nothing to me. My life shall be spent as their devoted enemy."

Then out came the story of the great conspiracy. The man's bitterness seemed to consume him.

"Hues, I will tell you a secret that belongs to my clan, which is of more importance than stealing negroes — a shorter way to an overgrown fortune, and it is not far ahead. The movements of my clan have been as brisk as I could expect in that matter; things are moving on smooth and easy." His voice lowered, as a man's will when he tells of something very dear to him. "But this is a matter that is known only by a few of our leading characters. The clan are not all of the same grit.

"The first class, which we call the Grand Council, keep all their designs and the extent of their plans to themselves. There are good reasons for this. All who are willing to join us are not capable of managing our designs; and there would be danger of their making disclosures which would lead to the destruction of our designs before they were perfected."

Stewart had wondered about that.

"The second class are those whom we trust with nothing except what they are immediately concerned with. We have them do what we are not willing to do ourselves. They always stand between us and danger. For a few dollars we can get one of them to run a negro, or a fine horse, to some place where we can go and take possession of it without any danger; and there is no danger in this fellow then, for he has become the offender, and of course he is bound to secrecy. This class are what we term the strikers. We have about four hundred of the Grand Council, and nearly six hundred and fifty strikers. I will give you a list of their names before we part."

At that promise Stewart felt that he might be getting somewhere. If he could get a list of names of these clansmen, he would have evidence. His mission was turning out to be something much larger than he had expected.

"The grand object that we have in contemplation is to excite a rebellion among the negroes throughout the slave-holding states," Murrell continued.

At last the definite scheme was out. Stewart shuddered. Surely the man must be mad!

"Our plan," Murrell continued, "is to have it commence everywhere at the same hour. We have set on the 25th of December, 1835, for the time to commence our operations. We design having our companies so stationed over the country, in the vicinities of the banks and large cities, and when the negroes commence their carnage and slaughter, we will have detachments to fire the towns and rob the banks while all is confusion and dismay. The rebellion taking place everywhere at the same time, every part of the country can afford no relief to another, until many places will be entirely overrun by the negroes, and our pockets replenished from the banks and desks of rich merchants' houses."

"But what about the places where the negroes were few?" Stewart asked.

"It is true that in many places in the slave states the negro population is not strong and would be easily overpowered; but back them with a few resolute leaders from our clan, they will murder thousands, and huddle the remainder into large bodies of stationary defence for their own preservation. And then, in many other places, the black population is much the strongest, and under a leader, would overrun the country before any steps could be taken to suppress them."

"I cannot see how the matter is made known to the negroes without endangering the scheme by a disclosure, as all the negroes are not disposed to see their owners murdered."

"That is very easily done," Murrell explained. We work on the proper materials, we do not go to every negro we see and tell him that the negroes intend to rebel on the night of the 25th of December, 1835. We find the most vicious and wickedly disposed on large farms, and poison their minds by telling them how they are mistreated, that they are entitled to their freedom as much as their masters, and that all the wealth of the country is the proceed of the black people's labor. We remind them of the pomp and splendor of their masters, and then refer them to their own degraded situation, and then tell them that it is power and tyranny which rivets their chains of bondage, and not their own inferiority to their masters. We tell them that all Europe has abandoned slavery, and that the West Indies are all free, and that they got their freedom by rebelling a few times and slaughtering the whites. We convince them that if they will follow the example of the West Indies negroes they will obtain their liberty, and become as much respected as if they were white. We tell them that they can marry white women when they are put on a level. In addition to this, we get them to believe that the free states in the United States would not interfere with the negroes if they were to butcher every white man in the slave-holding states."

Stewart thought of the Northern Abolitionists, their emotional anti-slavery propaganda and underground railroads organized to steal slaves from the masters and carry them away. In a sense, their purpose was not greatly unlike that of the clan, though there was a difference of motive and procedure. Murrell was overlooking nothing. He was taking advantage of the slavery feeling. It made the clansmen's work safer. Doubtless at no time in the history of the nation could such a diabolical scheme have

gotten under way better. But still Stewart could not believe that the man was not boasting.

Dark came and the men rode on into the night. Murrell explained with some triumph how they handled the
negroes. When some blood-thirsty black devil was found
who hated the whites, he was sworn to secrecy, and was
told something of the secrets of the organization. The
negroes were told that every other state and section of
the country, where there were any negroes, intended to
rebel at the same time. The negroes were put through
a long, weird ceremony for the oath, which was adminis-
tered in the presence of a hideous, impressive picture of
the devil, representing the monster who would deal with
them should they prove unfaithful. They were taught to
be obedient, and horrible penalties were cited for unfaith-
fulness.

"Our plan is to have the feelings of the negroes har-
rowed up against the whites, and their minds alive to
the idea of being free, and let none but such as we can
trust know the intention and time of rebellion until the
night it is to commence, when our black emissaries are to
have gatherings of their fellow slaves and invite all in
their reach to attend with the promise of plenty to drink,
which will always call negroes together. Our emissaries
will be furnished with money to procure spirits to give
them a few drams, when they will open their secrets as
follows: 'Fellow slaves, this is the night that we are to
obtain our liberty. All the negroes in America rebel this
night and murder the whites. We have long been subject
to the whips of our tyrants, and many of our backs wear
the scars; but the time has arrived when we can be re-
venged. There are many good white men who are helping us to gain our liberty. All of you who refuse to fight

will be put to death; so come on my brave fellows, we will be free or die.' "

It seemed that Murrell could talk of nothing but destruction. "We will have our men whom we intend for leaders ready to head those companies and encourage the negroes should they appear backward. Thus you see they will all be forced to engage, under the belief that all the negroes have rebelled everywhere else as in their own neighborhood, and by those means every gathering or assemblage of negroes will be pushed forward, even contrary to their inclination. The strikers will be of great use at the pinch of the game, as many of them will do to head the companies, and there will be no danger in them when they are to go immediately to work, and have the prospect of wealth before them; there are many of them who will fight like Turks."

Murrell explained how the blacks had been promised a share in the spoils. He said that his men always talked of victory and never defeat. "This may seem too bold to you, Hues; but that is what I glory in. All the crimes I have ever committed have been of the most daring; and I have been successful in all my attempts as yet; and I am confident that I will be victorious in this matter, as the robberies which I have in contemplation; and I will have the pleasure and honor of seeing and knowing that by my management I have glutted the earth with more human gore, and destroyed more human property, than any other robber who has lived in America, or the known world."

"But what if this plot should leak out?" Hues asked. He could not understand Murrell's calmness and cocksureness.

"In this matter, Hues, I have the advantage of any other leader of banditti that has ever preceded me. For at least one-half of my Grand Council are men of high standing, and many of them in high and lucrative offices. Should anything leak out by chance, these men would crush it at once, by ridiculing the idea and the fears of the people. They would soon make it a humbug, a cock-and-bull story; and all things would be accounted for to the satisfaction of the community in short order. These fellows make strong pillars in our mystic mansion."

"I cannot see how you will provide the negroes the arms to fight with," Hues said.

"We have a considerable amount of money in the hands of our treasurer for the purpose of purchasing arms and ammunition to fit out the armies that are to attack the cities and banks; and we will manage to get possession of different arsenals, and supply ourselves from every source that may offer. We can get from every house we enter more or less supplies of this kind until we will be well supplied. The negroes that will scour the country settlements will not want many arms until they can get them from the houses they destroy, as an axe, a club, or knife will do to murder a family at a late hour in the night, when all are sleeping. There will be but little defence made the first night by the country people, as all will be confusion and alarm for the first day or two, until the whites can embody."

Murrell talked, and rode on through the cold as a man with a superhuman power, warmed by his own passions and pushed on as if by some mad instinct. Stewart shook in his saddle, his legs ached; he felt as if he might be frost-bitten. He insisted on seeking lodging; he knew he could not ride all night. It was bitter cold. Murrell consented, though he had never complained, nor seemed to feel the effects of the keen, cutting wind that had been blowing all night.

At the first house that the travelers found, they

stopped and asked for lodging for the night. They warmed themselves by a blazing fire, and shortly retired for the night.

The night proved most disagreeable. There was not enough cover, the bed was hard, and the sharp wind came whistling through the gaping cracks of the crude country home, cutting the men like knives. Murrell rolled and tossed and cursed the host all night. There was little sleeping to be done. Stewart feared Murrell's temper. He might fly into a fit of rage and murder the man in cold blood. He was ill at ease about his notes, though he felt that they were in the safest possible place. He had cut the leaves out of his note book and placed them in the lining of his hat.

The men arose early the next morning and were riding before the sun was up. It was just as comfortable riding as it was trying to sleep in the hard bed without enough cover.

Murrell showed no signs of fatigue, though occasionally he directed an oath at the farmer who had "stalled them a shuck pen." The thought of getting to Arkansas stimulated Murrell. "By God, I'll make a man of you," he said to Stewart.

Murrell was talkative again. He told Stewart of his early life, how he had been taught to steal by his mother. He made a few funny remarks about the "old man" and his attempts at being a good man; and in rambling reminiscences the man gave a synopsis of his life. He told of horrible experiences he had had along the trace, as horrible crimes as the imagination could conceive. The man delighted in talking about himself. Stewart listened and tried to understand his strange companion. But it was a bewildering, startling thing to think about.

Toward night they were forced to leave the trace and change their route. The Mississippi River was overflowing, and backwater had the smaller streams out of their banks. The men worked toward the north. Murrell wanted to reach a private crossing place of the clan. But it soon became impossible to travel further up the river. So they were forced to spend the night on the Tennessee side of the river. Murrell cursed the luck, and raved about his delay. But he soon quieted. He was a man who could bow to circumstance as well as take advantage of it. They put up for the night at the home of a man by the name of John Champion, whose house stood on high ground just back from the Mississippi River.

The men had an early supper and soon were seated before a comfortable, blazing fire. Murrell, as usual, was brilliant in his conversation. Mr. Champion was impressed. The charming guest made inquiries of certain men along the Mississippi River — members of his clan — asking what standing they occupied as honorable and honest men. He was an utter stranger, but contemplated doing some business with them. Among other things he would like to know if their credit was good. He represented himself as a prosperous negro-trader. These neighbors of whom he had inquired were prospective buyers, he explained.

Murrell inquired of conditions in general, as is common with travelers. Were the outlaws bothering? Were any negroes being lost? Then, with all his art for entertainment, he began telling of conditions further east, and particularly what he had heard of those shrewd devils from Madison County. But Mr. Champion was not dazzled by the brilliant accomplishments of the dashing young fellows from Madison County. He expressed his contempt. "Something ought to be done about such things!"

"As I was going to say . . ." Murrell cut in hastily.
He changed the subject to religion.

The next morning Stewart felt a strange, more grip-
ping fear than he had as yet experienced. Once across
the river and he would be among the whole blood-thirsty
band of outlaws. He might not fool the others as easily
as he had fooled Murrell. He could not be sure yet that
Murrell was not leading him into a trap to be slaughtered
before the whole blood-loving mob. Once on the other side
force would be futile on his part. He would have to de-
pend, as he had in the past, entirely upon his wits. There
was little he could do about the situation now.

They were forced to leave their horses with Mr. Champion. They would have to travel on foot until they could
find a boat to ferry them across the river. And so as soon
as there was light enough to see they set out toward the
swamp. They had traveled about a half mile when Stewart
stopped suddenly. He told Murrell he had forgotten his
gloves. It was too cold to go on without them. If he would
do him the kindness to wait a few minutes he would rush
back and get them. It would not take long. Murrell said
that he would wait; and Stewart hurried off toward the
house.

Half out of breath Stewart told Champion what was
going on. He felt that he had to tell someone. If he went
into Arkansas he might never return. Then this terrible
plot for a negro rebellion would never be known until it
was too late. He told Champion of Parson Henning. If
he didn't return he asked that the parson and his family
be given some word of what had happened. If Murrell
returned for his horse without him it would be evidence
that he had been murdered or confined by the clan. If
such proved the case Champion could then cause Murrell's

arrest when he returned. Stewart was hurrying his words. Excitedly he blurted out his startling story of negro-running, rebellion, and robbery. He was afraid that Champion would think he was mad. But he had to risk it. He had to trust Champion. There seemed to be too much for Champion to grasp quickly. He was startled. It all made him nervous. He told Stewart that he could raise a guard of fifty men, perhaps only half knowing what he was saying. It was too late for that, Stewart told him; and then they must have evidence.

And then still blurting out his incoherent tale, he scurried off again toward the swamp where he had left Murrell. He found him seated on a log. He appeared impatient, but he made no fuss about it.

Backwater had the clan's private ferry cut off. They set out for the house of a certain Mr. Erwin, who Champion had told them lived on the other side of the swamp. The bottom was a muddy, half-frozen, sloppy mess. They bogged and stumbled on. Murrell was a powerhouse of driving enery. He never seemed to bother.

When they got to Erwin's they found more trouble. Erwin had been using a skiff, but it was borrowed and had been returned to its owner, who lived three miles down the river. Worse still, there was a lake between Erwin's place and that of the Reverend Hargus, the owner of the boat. And there was no available way of crossing it.

They were compelled to stop at the home of Mr. Erwin until they could find some way to cross either the lake or the river.

At Erwin's plantation, as at Champion's, Murrell spoke of himself as a negro trader, and by his captivating demeanor soon gained the confidence of his host. In a short time he had contracted with Mr. Erwin for three negro men to be delivered within three weeks at a price of three hundred dollars each.

They stayed at Mr. Erwin's house until the next afternoon, when a small trading-boat landed at the wood yard. The men secured passage as far down the river as the Reverend Hargus' place.

Erwin had been commended to Stewart by Mr. Champion. And before leaving Stewart appraised Erwin of his mission.

In late afternoon they landed at the house of Parson Hargus. The parson was courteous. Yes, they were welcome to the skiff, but it had been brought home for repairs; he would be much afraid to cross the river in it at that stage. Murrell announced that he would repair it himself, and he set out furiously at the task. But night came on before the job was near finished. There was nothing to do except spend the night with Parson Hargus.

The delay proved more extended than either of the men had expected. For next morning a storm was raging. The wind blew violently; the waves piled up high on the river; and then a heavy snow began to fall which continued all day and into the following night.

Murrell was impatient now. This was too much! During the day he frequently stepped out of the house eagerly looking for some sign of change in the weather. He stood by the river watching the waves roll high. He raved and cursed and swore that "the devil had ceased to cut his cards for him," and insisted that "the damn preacher's negroes had cost him more trouble than any he had ever stolen." But in all his excitement he never let one imprudent word slip in the presence of his host.

In the home of Parson Hargus he never ventured his subject of crime. He dwelt instead "with peculiar emphasis and animation on the great advantages of a moral and

religious education, and the happy effects of a general dif-
fusion of religious intelligence."

Murrell's ill fortune constantly brought Richard Henning to his mind. He told Stewart of a plan he already
had on foot to make Henning feel the consequence of the
free use he had been making of his and his brother's name.
A number of friends would go to the young upstart's house
some night, "take him from his bed, and give him two hundred and fifty lashes." Murrell himself would be lodging
at a hotel in Jackson that night. He planned to intrust
the task to one of his favored men whom he pronounced
"a second Caesar."

Redrawn from Wood Cut in "Life of Murrell"
MURRELL AND STEWART CROSSING THE MISSISSIPPI RIVER

The morning of February 1 presented almost as
gloomy prospects as the day before. The waves still rolled
high and threatening, and the snow continued to fall,
though in less quantities. Murrell became more determined.

He would cross the damn river anyway. A little more hammering and patching on the old skiff, and he called Stewart and they pushed the rickety thing into the raging stream. The boat surged and swerved down stream. A lashing wave piled into it. For a moment it seemed that all would go down. The men pulled furiously at the oars. They tried for the far shore, but they could do nothing against the current. Three miles down the stream they ran the old hull into the east bank; and the men fell out, exhausted and perspiring.

Later they found an old man who agreed to let his son take them across in a canoe. They finally landed at a point "on the western shore of the river opposite the mouth of Old River, which joins the Mississippi at the Chickasaw Bend."

At last they had reached Arkansas!

It was a desolate wilderness swamp into which Stewart and Murrell landed. Cane-breaks and swamp willows spread out as far as the eye could see. It appeared a hopeless, gloomy meaningless waste to Stewart. But Murrell steadied himself a moment, looked around, discovered a dim trail that no one else would have seen, and plunged on. Stewart followed blindly, fighting the swaying, cutting cane out of his face, stumbling over drift wood, bogging to his shoe tops. Crazily the men wandered on through the dim, misty silence of the dense Arkansas swamp.

They came to a small, dismal hut with smoke curling from a mud chimney. Stewart's heart pounded. "This must be the place where Henning's negroes are hidden," he thought. He fell behind and cocked both pistols. He muffled his face as much as possible with his top coat. The cabin they entered was a fearful, nasty hovel. They found two white men and two greasy-faced negroes eating

together at a rough table with their hands. But the negroes were not Henning's. Stewart was relieved.

Murrell knew one of the men. The man saluted him;
and Murrell called him by the name of Rainhart. He was
a huge, wild-looking, bearded man who swayed from side
to side as he walked, gorilla-like. The big man followed
Murrell out of the shanty. He called him aside and mumbled words that Stewart could not understand. They said
something about meeting at the council house the next day.
Stewart heard that.

Again they pushed on through the mud and thick undergrowth. They came to a lake, and Murrell sauntered
off to look for a boat. Shortly he called; he had found
one. They heaved off from the bank into the muddy lake.
It was a large body of water that opened into several
bayous. Presently Murrell left the lake and paddled up
one of the larger streams.

On the bank of the bayou they found another small,
filthy cabin which proved to be the wretched home of a
white man and his family. Again Stewart feared coming
into contact with the parson's negroes. The occupants
were different from the last. Inside was a man, his wife
and two children, who sat in drowsy silence by the fire.
Murrell knew them. They spoke with no signs of enthusiasm. Murrell borrowed a lighter boat to cross a stream
further on, and was off again without losing time.

They traveled on until they came to a small clearing,
and in it was a crudely constructed camp. In the camp
they found seated three negroes "alone and cheerless, in
filthy attire . . . with the melancholy pensiveness of des-
ponding criminals." There was no white person about.
Murrell inquired what had become of their leader, and
they answered that they had not seen him for several days.

The men pressed on again into the dreary silent

swamp. To Stewart it seemed a country of the damned. What manner of creatures would live here? It made him feel sick.

They reached a spot of ground where the cane was not so thick. Murrell looked about. Then he called Stewart closely to him, and pointed out over the morass. "Do you see yonder cottonwood tree that towers over all the other trees?"

"Yes," Stewart responded, wondering what next!

"That tree," said Murrell, "stands in the Garden of Eden. That is headquarters of our clan!"

Chapter XIII

THE CLAN

A N air of "peculiar solemnity and gloom" surrounded the solitary house that was the clan's headquarters. It was a large, low building crudely constructed of logs from the woods. There was a long room and several smaller chambers that opened into it along the back side. It was a poorly furnished, filthy-looking place that "reeked of sweat, stale whiskey, leather and manure." It was a place such as only filthy men of low breeding would have kept. In the large room were a long trestle table and a few scattered chairs. Around the walls were crudely improvised shelves that held nasty-looking bottles and cans. Pegs driven into the walls held saddles, bridles, saddle bags, holsters, shot pouches; damp and mildewed clothing hung in careless fashion. The ground served as a floor.

The timber and canebreaks crowded closely in upon the house. A few yards away was a shallow lake with banks covered with bushes and canes. The place appeared to Stewart as a strange, lost den.

They found eleven men at the council house huddled around the fireplace before a smoldering fire. The men saluted their chief and made way for him and Stewart at the fire. Later, more men began to drift in, as the news spread that the chief had arrived. It was not long before the big room was almost full.

MURRELL AT CLAN HEADQUARTERS

The room was astir. The men came in and saluted each other in peculiar fashion. Murrell was not satisfied with the number present. Why were there not more men present! They explained that some had remained at home because of the hard season; and then some had come and gone away again, thinking that Murrell had decided not to come. The gang had been bothered about him!

Then they inquired the cause of their chief's delay.

Murrell fell to cursing. He explained how "that damned old preacher's negroes" had given him more trouble than any he had ever handled, and how the parson's talk had caused him to be delayed. He told them what a "hell of a time" he had crossing the river.

His followers informed him that the negroes had arrived some days before and were badly frosted. The men in charge had become doubtful as to the time of his return and they had thought it best to push the slaves and make sales as soon as possible. They had sent the parson's two negroes with two others and seven horses down the river on a trading boat to the Yazoo market. Incidentally the men in charge had been given several thousand dollars in counterfeit to dispose of along the way. Murrell nodded his approval, slowly.

There was drinking and vulgar stories and much guffawing among the men. Then Murrell called the house to order and presented Stewart to the fraternity. "This is a councillor of my own making," he said, "and I am not ashamed of the workmanship; let Hues be examined by whom he may." The mystic Grand Council went into session and Hues was arranged for the ceremonies.

A peculiar air of childish mystery accompanied the awkward ceremonies. Silly they seemed! But they appealed to the simple minds of these backwoods ruffians. They delighted in the strained half-carried formalities that mocked pomp and grace. They gave the candidate the two degrees, and the signs, which belonged to the two classes of members. He first received the sign of the striker, and afterwards, that of the Grand Councillor.

"The first mystic sign which was used by the clan," Murrell explained to Stewart, "was in use among robbers before I was born." The second sign was originated by Murrell and a few friends in New Orleans. "We needed a higher order to carry on our designs, and we adopted our sign, and called it the sign of the Grand Council of the mystic clan. . . . We practiced ourselves to give and receive the new sign to a fraction before we parted." The outlaws also had a handshake which was done with the fingers closed against the palm.

After the ceremonies all the members shook hands with Stewart. He "was drilled by them in giving and receiving these signs till he could equal the most skillful."

Then came the regular business of the order to be transacted, all carried out in solemn lodge fashion. Murrell presided. What progress had been made in the distribution of counterfeit money? What new speculations had been made? Were any members of the fraternity overtaken or in prison, and needed their assistance? How many proselytes had been made to the cause? Were there other candidates for admission? It went on for hours.

Late in the day Murrell and Stewart broke away from the gang at the council house. Murrell had business elsewhere to attend, and he wanted to show Stewart the lay of the land. Stewart was glad to get away. He had lived for hours not knowing what the next minute might bring. It all seemed like a horrible dream. He felt better in the open air again, away from the sickening stench of the damp, overcrowded council house.

They set out through the swamp to the house of a certain Jehu Barney. On the way they passed a small hut where four negroes were cutting wood. Murrell remarked that those negroes had been stolen several times and were still in reserve for a future market. They made no halt, but passed on.

On the edge of a bayou they passed a flatboat of considerable size, which appeared to be undergoing repair. Murrell explained that it was his own. He said that he intended it to convey negroes to some point on the river below New Orleans. From there the negroes could be shipped to Texas, at the shortest notice, on board a packet.

He had already made arrangements for some forty or fifty negroes with that plan in view.

They, at length, arrived at the cabin of Jehu Barney. It was so late that they were compelled to spend the night in his miserable quarters.

During the conversation of the evening Stewart learned, among other things, of Murrell's arrangements for retaking the negroes he had promised to sell to Mr. Erwin. It was planned that Murrell should deliver the negroes as promised, and secure his money, leaving with the negroes directions to appear at a certain point on the river the following night. Barney was instructed to meet them there and convey them to another market.

Stewart also heard called the names of many members of the clan, who lived near the council house. Many of them owned huts and lived in the morass under the pretences of running ferries, wood-cutting or keeping wood yards for Mississippi boatmen. Stewart wondered how many there really were.

The night passed.

Stewart felt that he had to get away. He feared to tell Murrell. But he came out with it. Murrell was surprised. "What's the hurry?" he asked. They hadn't had any fun yet! He had not had time to redeem his promise to show him the Arkansas ladies. "You wait," Murrell insisted, "and I'll show you Arkansas yet." Furthermore there were important plans to be discussed at the council house that day.

Stewart suggested that his opinion would be of little importance before the council. He would leave his vote in Murrell's hands. Murrell was flattered. He quieted for a moment. But again he reminded Stewart of the plump Arkansas girls. They would have a regular frolic if he would stay!

Stewart edged over closer to Murrell. He didn't
know just how to say it. But he told Murrell that right
now he had rather see the pretty widow back at Erwin's
than any of the Arkansas girls. They could get to them
later. Murrell grinned, and squinted a mischievous eye
at him. "So that's the reason you want to go back!" Well
. . . he would see him at Erwin's then.

It was a bewildering, frightening tale that Stewart
related to Erwin at his home on the night of February 2nd.
But he told of his experiences and the terrible plans of
the clan until much of the night had passed. Something
would have to be done quickly! They planned that a
guard would be formed and concealed about the house when
Murrell came across from Arkansas with his slaves. In
this way they would catch him with the goods. Stewart
felt relieved. He felt proud of his efforts. Until now
his success had hung upon such a dangerously slender
thread! For eight days his life had been in jeopardy.
He had failed to get Henning's negroes, but he felt that
he had done a greater work.

Next day a guard of several men was hurriedly formed
and stationed about the house. They waited for Murrell.
Stewart relaxed.

Shortly after noon, someone sighted Murrell coming
up the trail that led from the river. The guards hid themselves; they stood at readiness with loaded guns. Further
on Murrell advanced until he was near the house. But
there were no slaves! The man was alone.

"Strange!" Stewart thought. He whispered to Erwin
again that he had heard Murrell discuss his plans two
nights before. He was sure of it.

Then a chilling thought came to Stewart. Maybe

someone had tipped Murrell off. Murrell had said there were many prominent men in his clan. Perhaps someone had spotted him and revealed his identity. But if so, why would the man be coming back in this manner! Then he thought how important it would be to the clan for him to be destroyed. But he was in no immediate danger now. He was surrounded by his friends, and they were armed.

Erwin was for having the guards rush out and capture the bandit at once; but Stewart insisted that it would never do. They must have evidence. They would wait and see.

Murrell approached. There were greetings in quite the usual manner. Everyone was tense. Murrell was apologetic. An unexpected mishap had caused him to have to delay the delivery of Mr. Erwin's negroes. But he promised that they would be delivered soon. Still Stewart was puzzled.

They would have to wait. Stewart gave a signal. The guards slipped away.

As soon as an opportunity offered, Stewart asked Murrell privately what had gone wrong. He found that below Murrell's mask of graceful manners, he was in a rotten humor. The man who had handled the negroes intended for Erwin had "sold them too damn fast and caused suspicion." They would have to be held over until the excitement could pass over. They had been entrusted to a striker.

Then affairs had not gone so well at the council meeting. The men who had carried the Henning negroes to the Yazoo market with the two other negroes and seven horses were only strikers. "You can't afford to trust the strikers too much," Murrell said. "That is too much to put in their hands at one time. Damned if I am not fearful they will think themselves made when they sell, and

leave us behind in the lurch. . . . I would have avoided that
if I had been there."

Stewart trusted Murrell's story. It seemed straight
enough. He would have to carry on. Murrell, after this
turn of fortune, was in a hurry to get back to Madison
County. Stewart excused himself. He told Murrell he
wanted to tell the pretty widow good-bye. Instead he
rushed to Erwin and hurriedly told him to keep the affair
a secret. There were too many prominent people in the
clan for the matter to be talked. They might wait and
catch Murrell when he came again to deliver the slaves.
It was agreed.

Murrell and Stewart set out for Champion's home
where their horses were stationed. They spent the night
there; and early next morning set out for Madison County.

All through the day of the 4th, the men rode back
toward Madison County. Murrell rattled on all day. He
liked to talk; perhaps for the pure art of it and to soothe
his vanity. And then this eager, boyish-faced companion
was such a good listener!

He told Stewart how he and a few friends had invented
a code of correspondence which they used when "any of
us get into difficulty." It consisted of "ten characters
mixed with other matter," and it had been "very convenient on many occasions."

He spoke of wealth he had in time possessed. "I have
frequently had money enough to settle myself in wealth,
but I have spent it as freely as water in carrying out my
designs."

They passed a beautiful pasture of fine, well-bred
horses. Murrell had to admire them. A good piece of
horse flesh never failed to have its appeal for him. It re-

minded him of the times when he did lots of horse stealing. He told of one of the tricks "they" used:

A friend examined the stray books regularly, and whenever a stray horse of any value was found recorded on them he would go and get a description of the horse. Then if he had no friends near who were strangers in the community, he would write or send for two associates. When the friends came he would give them a minute description of the horse, and one would go and claim the horse and the other prove the property. It was just another cunning scheme Murrell had devised to take advantage of the law. "A man's a fool not to know the law," he emphasized again.

He told Stewart of a recent example in Arkansas: "I was in Arkansas this fall," he said, "and there was a man there who had found a fine horse standing in the edge of the Mississippi River, which had probably got off some boat and swum to the shore, but he could not get up the bank. The man dug the bank away and saved the horse. One of my friends heard of it, and went and examined the horse, and told me all of his flesh marks. I went and asked the man if he had found a horse of such description, describing the horse in every particular. He said he had. I gave the fellow five dollars for his trouble, and took him home. And I have him yet. I have swum the Mississippi twice on that horse."

There seemed to be no end to Murrell's escapades. The mere relating of them kindled his flaming passion to do huge things. To admire him, or marvel at his accomplishments was to refresh a burning thirst. He spoke of vengeance, of "scenes of devastation, smoked walls and fragments." At times the man became rhetorical.

"Hues, I want you to be with me at New Orleans on the night that the negroes commence their ravages," he said. "I intend to head the company that attacks that city myself. I feel an ambition to demolish that city."

"Such bitterness!" Stewart thought. But what was worse: What a morbid ambition!

"I shall glory in that," he said, clenching his saddle horn passionately. "By God, Hues, even the British couldn't take it!"

February 5th was the day of parting. Much against Murrell's pleas, Stewart insisted that he must hasten to the Choctaw Nation to see after his business there. But he promised that he would hurry, and as soon as he had finished he would rejoin Murrell at his home in Madison County.

A short distance from the town of Wesley the men turned off the road for a couple of hundred yards. There was some last minute business that had been forgotten! Murrell had a number of important deals under way:

"I have forty negroes now engaged that are waiting for me to run them . . . and the best of it is, they are almost all the property of my enemies." He spoke of the great number of friends who "have got in to be overseers." A certain Nolan in Alabama, "my brother-in-law's brother," was one of these overseers—and the owner was at present away from home. It proved a very advantageous situation. Already he had decoyed "six likely negroes" away. He told Stewart how he would handle these darkies. According to plan he would go within ten miles of the place with a two-horse carryall, and stop at an appointed place. "Nolan is to raise a sham charge against the negroes and they are to run off and come to my wagon." Then all would be easy enough. They would be put in the wagon, fodder thrown over them, and the curtains drawn down all around. A striker would drive them to the Mississippi swamp. Murrell would ride a few miles behind, but never seem to notice the wagon. "Nolan is to be driving the woods for the negroes, and reporting that he has seen them every day or two, until I have had time to get clear out of the country with them."

Murrell spoke of eight more slaves he had engaged in Alabama at the house of a certain Eason. The remainder of the forty he would get in his own county. "You recollect the boat I showed you in the bayou on the other side of the river?" he asked Stewart. "That boat I intend to fill with negroes for my own benefit." He was letting Stewart in on his private business. He had promised him that he would show him a quick way to fortune and he was going to do it.

Stewart reminded Murrell that he had not as yet given him the list of the names of the clan as promised. Murrell asked if he had paper. He did, but he found that he had only a small amount. Murrell told him that he did not have near enough when he saw what he had on hand. He told Stewart to wait until he came over home, and he would write out a complete list.

But Stewart insisted that he give him a list of the principal characters in the different sections of the country. He wanted to form some idea of the strength of the clan, and to familiarize himself with the names. He suggested, in order to save space, that only the initial of the christian name be given. (*See note at end of chapter.*)

Murrell agreed. And little did either of the men dream what trouble this list would bring to both of them as well as others!

At Wesley the men parted. Murrell headed out over the regular road to Madison County. Stewart headed toward the Choctaw Nation. But as soon as Murrell was out of sight Stewart turned sharply and set out over another route for Madison County.

When Stewart told his story in Madison County it spread like wild fire. Citizens became infuriated. They almost lost their sense of reason. "So that's the way our slaves have been going!" they said. It was almost too good to have this negro thief walk right into their hands. But they acted too hastily. It threw Stewart into a strained situation. He had planned to capture Murrell at Erwin's when he came to deliver the negroes, so that he might be taken with stolen property actually in his possession. But the infuriated farmers would take no such chance. They had suspected him long before. The man was shrewd. They might never get the opportunity again.

The only evidence now against Murrell was the testimony of Stewart himself. Stewart regretted this. But his plan was voted down. The men were determined to capture Murrell at once.

NOTE

A pamphlet issued on the authority of the City Council of New Orleans was distributed throughout Louisiana to apprise the inhabitants of the State of the Murell-gang danger. The pamphlet quoted Murel as setting December 25, 1835 as the date for the slave rebellion.

It was dated "Council Chamber, New Orleans, August 1, 1835", and was signed by A. W. Pichot, Chairman, J. S. McFarlane and Joshua Baldwin. A rare copy of this pamphlet is now in possession of the Howard Library at New Orleans and the following list of names is quoted from it:

CATALOGUE OF MUREL'S MYSTIC CLAN

TENNESSEE
Two—Murrels'
S. Wethers
S. Spiers
Two—Byrdsongs'
D. Crenshaw
M. Dickson
V. Chisim
Col. Jarot
Two—Nolins'
Capt. Ruffin
K. Dickson
L. Anderson
P. Johnson
J. Nuckels
L. Bateman
J. Taylor
E. Chandlor
Four—Maroneys'
Two—Littlepages'
J. Hardin
Esq. Wilbern
Y. Pearson
G. Wiers
Five—Lathoms'
A. Smith
Six—Hueses'
Ja. Hosskins
W. Crenshaw
J. Goaldin
R. Tims
D. Ahart
Two—Busbeys'
L. More
J. Eas
W. Howel
B. Sims
Z. Gorin
Three—Boaltons'
G. Sparkes
S. Larit
R. Parew
K. Deron

MISSISSIPPI

G. Parker
S. Williams
R. Horton

W. Presley
C. Hopes
G. Corkle
B. Johnson
D. Rooker
L. Cooper
C. Darton
Five—Willeys'
J. Hess
Two—Willsons'
Capt. Moris
G. Tucker
Three—Glenns'
Two—Harlins'
——Bloodworth
J. Durham
R. Forrow
S. Cook
G. Goodman
——Stantton
——Clavin
C. Hickman
W. Thomas
Wm. Nawls
D. Marlow
Capt. Medford
Three—Hunters'
Two—Gilberts'
A. Brown
Four—Yarbers'

ARKANSAW

S. Pucket
W. Ray
J. Simmons
L. Good
B. Norton
J. Smith
P. Billing
A. Hooper
C. Jimerson
Six—Serrils'
Three—Bunches'
Four—Dartes'
Two—Barneys'
G. Aker
Four—Tuckers

Two—Loyds'
Three—Spurlocks'
Three—Joneses'
L. Martih
S. Coulter
H. Petit
W. Hendorson
Two—Nowlins'
Three—Hortons'

KENTUCKY

Three—Forrows'
Four—Wards'
Two—Foresytes'
D. Clayton
R. Williamson
H. Haly
H. Potter
D. Mugit
Two—Pattersons'
S. Goin
Q. Brantley
L. Pots
Four—Reeses'
Two—Carters'

MISSOURI
Four—Whites'
Two—Herins'
Six—Milers'
G. Poap
R. Coward
D. Corkle
E. Boalin
W. Aker
Two—Garlins'
S. Falcon
H. Warrin
Two—Moaseways'
Three—Johsons'
Col. S. W. Foreman

ALABAMA

H. Write
J. Homes
G. Sheridon
E. Nolin
Three—Parmers'

Two—Glascocks'
G. Hammons
R. Cunagen
H. Chance
D. Belfer
W. Hickel
P. Miles
O. More
B. Corhoon
S. Baley
Four—Sorils'
Three—Martins'
H. Hancock
Capt. Boin
Esq. Malone

GEORGIA

H. Moris
D. Harris
Two—Rameys'
Four—Cullins'
W. Johnson
S. Gambel
Two—Crenshaws'
Four—Peakes'
Two—Heffis'
D. Coalmon
Four—Reves'
Six—Rosses'
Capt. Ashley
Denson, Esq.
Two—Lenits'

SOUTH CAROLINA

Three—Foats
Four—Williamses'
O. Russet
S. Pinkney
Six—Woods'
H. Black
G. Holler
Three—Franklins'
W. Simpson
E. Owin
Two—Hookers
Three—Piles'
W. King
N. Parsons
F. Watters

M. Ware
G. Gravit
B. Henry
Two—Robersons'

NORTH CAROLINA

A. Fentres
Two—Micklejohns'
D. Harrilson
M. Coopwood
R. Huiston
Four—Solomons'
J. Hackney
S. Stogdon
Three—Perrys'
Four—Gilferds'
W. Pariners
Three—Hacks'
J. Secel
D. Barnet
S. Bulkes
M. Johnson
B. Kelit
V. Miles
J. Haris
L. Smith
K. Farmer

VIRGINIA

R. Garison
A. Beloach
J. Kerkmon
Three—Merits'
W. Carnes
D. Hawks
P. Hume
F. Henderson
J. Ferines
G. Derom
S. Walker
Four—Mathises'
L. Wiseman
S. Washborn
E. Cockburn
W. Milbern

MARYLAND

W. Gwins
H. Brown

F. Smith
G. Dotherd
S. Strawn
Three—Morgans'
D. Hayes
Four—Hobees'
H. McGleton
S. McWrite
J. Wilkit
Two—Fishers'
M. Hains
C. Paron
G. McWatters
A. Cuthbut
W. Leemon
S. Winston
D. Read
M. O'Conel
T. Goodin

FLORIDA

E. Carmeter
W. Hargeret
S. Whipel
A. Sterling
B. Stafford
L. McGuint
G. Flush
C. Winkle
Two—McGillits'
E. Foshew
J. Beark
J. Preston
Three—Baggets'

LOUISIANA

C. Deport
J. Bevley
J. Johnson
A. Pelkin
A. Rhone
T. McNut
H. Pelton
W. Bryant
Four—Hunts'
Two—Baleys'
S. Roberson
J. Sims
G. Murry

R. Miler
C. Henderson
Two—Derris'
D. Willis
P. Read

S. McCarty
W. Moss
D. Cotton
F. Parker
L. Ducan

M. Bluren
S. Muret
G. Pase
T. Ray

Transients, Who Travel from Place to Place

Two—Hains'
S. Coper
G. Boalton
R. Haris
P. Doddrige
H. Helley

C. Moris
Three—Rinens'
L. Tailor
Two—Jones'
H. Sparkes

Three—Levits'
G. Hunter
G. Tucker
S. Skerlock
Soril Phelps

CHAPTER XIV

MISTAKE OF HASTE

WHEN Murrell rode up to his plantation on the evening of the 7th a group of armed men were waiting for him. They surrounded him with pointed guns.

But Murrell was calm. He made no display of emotion. He had seen these things before.

They showered questions at him as eager, nervous men will do when they are scared, or not sure of themselves: Where had he been? Over in Arkansas, the answer came, with cool confidence—on business. Alone? No, a young fellow named Hues had traveled most of the way with him. Did he know this man before? No, he met him on the way—over near Estanaula.

The man's bold face and air of cocksureness were remarkable. He knew how to play a bold part. But the Tennessee farmers also felt sure of themselves this time. An officer called for Mr. Hues; and Mr. Hues came brushing his way through the crowd.

If Murrell had suddenly seen a man raised from the dead he could probably have looked no worse. "His countenance fell . . . his self-possession and firmness forsook him. He once came near swooning away."

They conducted him, under heavy guard, to the county jail at Jackson. On the road he recovered some of his self-possession. He asked one of the guards who this man Hues was and whether or not he had many acquaintances in the country.

The guards had been asked not to expose Stewart's identity. And so they told him that Hues was a stranger to them.

"Well," said Murrell, "he had better remain a stranger. I have friends. I had much rather be in my condition than his."

They lodged Murrell behind the bars of the county jail at Jackson to await trial. The sheriff and prominent citizens of the county set out to find some collaboration for Stewart's testimony.

The news of Murrell's capture spread rapidly all over east Tennessee and along the Mississippi River. The notorious Murrell had been captured: It was a subject that conjured up many tales. Men along the Mississippi retold stories of unsolved crimes that had baffled and shaken the river towns with horror. "It was those terrible Murrells:" they said now.

For years the law along the Mississippi wilderness had been just strong enough to make crime interesting. About the time Murrell was born the Spanish government had taken steps to suppress organized gangs along the Mississippi River. From the Ohio to the mouth of the river these marauders played havoc with transportation until the very existence of Spanish commerce was threatened. The outlaws appeared singly and in gangs, and they grew in number as transportation and commerce in-

creased. Many bold bandits made names in the valley
never to be forgotten.

Then Murrell came strutting out from the middle
Tennessee hills to the River where life was faster, more
dangerous and reckless. He determined to outdo them all.

The secert of his success lay chiefly in the fact that
he made it a rule never to rob a man without murdering
him. He never let the man live who might bear evidence
against him. Then, the risky, open work of the clan was
done mainly by strikers, who did not know the extent of
their own gang, and who, most of the time, did not know
the men who were promoting their exploits.

Now that the terrible Murrell had been captured and
his plans exposed, the country was soon buzzing with accounts of murders and thefts and robberies. Many old,
almost-forgotten stories of terrible crimes were retold and
speculated upon. One crime in particular was reviewed.
There had always been some doubt about it, but now that
it was known that Murrell headed a vast gang, people felt
sure that it was his bloody work: The entire crew of
a flatboat had been murdered in cold blood, disemboweled,
and their loaded corpses thrown splashing into the river.
The outlaws had taken all the money and goods from the
boat and vanished into the swamps. The Murrell gang
was charged with the fearful deed; and public meetings
were called in different parts of the country to devise
some means to rid the country and clear the woods of this
hellish band. Companies were formed for the purpose of
apprehending and bringing these men to justice. One was
formed at Covington under the command of Major Hock-
ley and Granville De Searcy. Another was formed at Randolph, under the command of Colonel Orville Shelby. They
met at Randolph and organized into one company under
the command of Colonel Shelby. They were determined

to capture this bloodthirsty bandit if it was the last act of their lives.

A flatboat was secured for the expedition. It was loaded with arms, and sufficient rations to last for several days. When it shoved off from Randolph some eighty or a hundred determined men were on board. They floated down the river to the place where the wholesale murder had been committed. There they tied up at the bank, shouldered their arms, and set out for Shawnee Village, Arkansas, where the sheriff of the county lived. They were going to require the sheriff to put the criminals under arrest and then turn them over to them to be dealt with according to the law.

The expedition set out to Shawnee Village, moving in single file, along a tortuous trail through cane and jungle. Suddenly the whole line was startled by a shrill whistle near the head of the column, answered by a sharp click, click, click of cocking rifles somewhere in the cane.

Then the leader (though not Murrell) pushed through the cane and stepped out in plain sight of the troops. He raised his hand and shouted a command at the expedition to halt. "We have man for man, move forward another step and a rifle ball will be sent through every man in your command." A parley was held; the ruffians rose from their hiding places in the matted cane and grass, their guns in position for action.

The posse had marched into a trap. The outlaws had learned of the movement against them. Doubtless many of them had set in the meeting that had planned their destruction. There was nothing that the posse could do except accept their failure.

The expedition made its way slowly back to the river, a beaten bunch of disheartened men. There was disappointment at Randolph when the men returned empty-handed. They had left with such confidence and determination.

Leaders of the posse communicated with the sheriff of that county. The officer promised that he would do what he could in having the offenders brought to justice.

The people of Randolph awaited some action of the sheriff. He made promises. But he never produced a man. Time dragged on. Then the people accused the sheriff of being in sympathy with the gang. Probably they were right. And it is equally as probable that they were wrong. The Valley had not yet learned of the cleverness of John A. Murrell.

Posse after posse were sent after the law breakers in the swamp. It was believed that Murrell headed the outlaws, but still there was no direct evidence against him. It became a common proverb to speak of a man "as slick as Murrell." Detectives, sheriffs and detachments of Federal troops pursued him at times, but all to no purpose.

Finally depredations became so bad in southeastern Arkansas that the governor called upon a West Pointer by the name of Colonel Moore to hunt Murrell and "run him to earth." Colonel Moore rubbed up his sword, mounted his horse and gave the command "fall in." The hunt began in Lee County. From swamp to swamp, through valley and forest the hunt went on from day to day. When they thought they had Murrell cornered they would hear of some wild raid taking place in some other part of the country; and the hunt would begin anew. It seemed that the clan chief was playing a game of fox and hound. But it was a devilish game. These smart tricks were too much for the pompous Colonel Moore, and finally he turned in disgust to the shriff saying: "What kind of man is this Murrell?"

"He is a regular devil, Colonel," replied the sheriff.

"Then I wish he was in hell," said the outdone West Point warrior. And he gave the command for the homeward march.

The evading fox had enjoyed a very entertaining season. The vain, handsome bandit chuckled long over the reports that his lieutenants sent him. It was a merry game, such as always delighted the crafty Murrell. Neither Colonel Moore, the governor, nor the sheriff knew the strength of the clan, nor that prominent citizens were members. Members of Murrell's clan were in the posse that was marching so diligently for him with the avowed determination to "run him to earth."

It seemed that Murrell might have been apprehended in Madison County at his home. But there he was a different man. During the heated days he was only darting in and out. No one could prove anything, nothing definite could be pinned on the outlaw, there was no evidence. And worse of all Murrell was beginning to be feared as if he was a ferocious beast. A few aggressive people like Richard Henning began to express suspicion. But no one could make a case against the man. It had been tried. Murrell was always slick enough to wiggle out. It was thought best in Madison County not to evoke his wrath.

Now that Murrell had talked and had been arrested, people told these stories over and over, and speculated upon many daring deeds of the Valley. They talked more freely and breathed easier. They wanted to believe that the terrible outlaw days were over.

While Murrell lay in jail, there was rejoicing in Madison County and along the Mississippi. The country felt relieved. People talked of that brave fellow Stewart.

Murrell soon gained his self-possession. He joked with the jailors, received visitors daily, and chatted with

his friends. It was a trivial affair, a technicality, he insisted. He played a bold part.

But the citizens of Madison County were not impressed
with his smooth talk. They were proud of their catch.
They now set out to find some collaboration for Stewart's
evidence.

A sheriff's posse rode down to the Mississippi and
crossed over into Arkansas. They took Stewart along to
make identifications. They searched the swamp from end
to end. They found the camp by the great council tree
where Stewart had met the mysterious, mystic clan. But
it was abandoned. There was no sign of life anywhere.
A warning had spread ahead of them through the clan's
underground channels, and all the men the posse sought
had set out for unknown parts.

A son of Parson Henning and a group of citizens rode
down the river in search of the slaves that had been sent
down for the Yazoo market. A boatman told them that,
at the time of which they spoke, Murrell's boat could not
have entered the pass. The water had been too high. Perhaps the negro-runners had changed their course and gone
on down the river. Young Henning took the suggestion
and proceeded alone to Vicksburg in search of the negroes.
Days later he returned home, worn out, disappointed,
puzzled. No one ever heard of the slaves again.

A group of irritated farmers kept watch at Erwin's
place. When the agent brought the slaves that Erwin had
contracted for, they would nab him. They waited and
waited. No one showed up.

Murrell was not the only man with troubles. Many
of the men on Stewart's list, Murrell had referred to as
"big bugs," men prominent in business and who "stood fair
in society." Stewart had not made his list public; he

planned to wait until after the trial to publish the list with Murrell's confessions. But the fact that Murrell had admitted giving Stewart a list of their names was maddening. Anxiety ran into hysteria. Respectable bankers had bidded for clansmen's accounts; traders and merchants had bought their goods without asking questions. Peace officers had been induced, either through money or fear to go blind at times; shyster lawyers had joined the clan because ignorant strikers frequently got caught with stray horses and needed legal help. There were good fees for defending them. Then there were eager men in general, anxious to make a quick and easy fortune, who had been tempted to tamper with this organization and mix a few easy, dishonest dollars with properly earned ones. They did no robbing or killing. It looked safe enough.

Now they were a nervous bunch, indeed. Something must be done; or they would all be ruined.

After all, the problem was clear enough. There were but two alternatives. The character of Stewart must be destroyed, or he would destroy them. Stewart was the state's only witness. There was only one solution; they must destroy his claim to credibility.

On the 21st of February Stewart returned to the little settlement in the Choctaw Purchase to attend to his long neglected business. He found it general known throughout the country that Murrell had been arrested. The country was buzzing with gossip. Vague rumors were floating about concerning prominent men who were suspected of being members of the clan.

But the clan had lost no time in starting their defensive campaign. The story was all a frame-up on the part of that upstart Stewart, the clansmen told the people. The whole affair would blow over in a short while. Nasty gossip was being passed around about Stewart. He recognized a change in conduct toward him among some of his friends. It all made him uncomfortable. He realized more than ever now that the farmers of Madison County had acted too hastily in arresting Murrell. Within ten days he left the Purchase and set out again for Madison County. He would feel better among his old friends.

Stewart's return to Madison County brought a fresh disappointment. Rumors of the most damning nature were circulating about him. Murrell had been busy in the Jackson jail. He was not bothered about the law, he told his friends. He knew more about it than most of the judges. And it stood him in good stead. He conferred with his friends. He wrote letters. He organized a plan of propaganda that might have ruined any character. Through his wife and associates he sent out suggestions as to how Stewart might be made incredible and his testimony ruined. First his character was to be attacked; and then the defendant's witnesses would prove more directly that Stewart had a personal interest in arresting Murrell, and was much concerned with the outcome of the trial from a standpoint of personal profit. To effect the point that Stewart had a personal interest in Murrell's arrest and the outcome of the trial he sent out the following letter in the form of a certificate, to indicate that Stewart had invented the whole thing in order to collect the reward:

"This day personally appeared before us, etc., Jahu Barney, James Tucker, Thomas Dark, Joseph Dark, Wm. Loyd, etc., who being sworn in due form of law, did depose and say that they were present and saw _____ Stewart of Yellow Busha in the evening of the first day of February last, in company with John Murrell, at the house of Jahu Barney, over the Mississippi River, and that he the said Stewart informed us that he was in pursuit of John

Murrell, for stealing two negro men from Preacher Henning and his son Richard, in Madison County, near Denmark, and that he told Murrell his name was Hues, and he wished us to call him Hues in Murrell's hearing. We also recollect to have heard him, the said Stewart, say distinctly that he was to get five hundred dollars for finding said negroes and causing Murrell to be convicted for them. But he did not say who was to give him the reward, but stated that he held the obligation of several rich men for that amount.

Signed ...."

Below this circular Murrell wrote:

"The above is a copy given to me, by one who heard him say it, in the presence of you all. You will therefore please send me the names of all that will testify these facts in writing. Also send me the names of all and every man that will certify these witnesses to be men of truth.

J. MURRELL."

Murrell sent out another circular letter to his friends:

". . . . . But above all things, arrest him . . . for passing the six twenty dollar bills. You will have to go out in Yellow Busha, in Yellow Busha County, near the centre, for him; and undoubtedly this matter will be worth your attention, for if it be one, two, or three hundred dollars, the gentleman to whom he passed it can present it before a magistrate and take a judgment for that amount, and his little provision store acc's etc., is worth that much money. . . . . My distressed wife will proably call on you, and if she does, you may answer all her requests without reserve.

Yours

J. MURRELL."

Soon the Valley and west Tennessee were alive with vile rumors about Stewart: His father had been a notorious horse thief in Georgia. His reputation had been so infamous that the son could not carry on there. Young Stewart had fought a boatman over a woman in the red light district in Vicksburg. It was a terrible, nasty affair; and the officers had run both the men out of town. Stewart was an "unblushing villain" who had tried to crash in on respectable society; he had been put off a river boat for cheating at cards; he had been arrested for forgery down the river; he was wanted for passing counterfeit in Alabama and Arkansas.

People asked when Stewart would publish his list. He said little about it. He began to feel that his life was not safe. On the first of April he left again for the Purchase. He decided that there he would be farther away from Murrell and his friends. Mr. Clanton and Vess would stick by him. His belongings were there. He would settle down quietly until the trial.

His arrival was a startling revelation. Conditions had become much worse for him here. It seemed that there was no end to his persecution, that there was no place where he could rest. It seemed that Stewart's lot was becoming worse than Murrell's. Vess greeted him at the cabin, but he appeared confused whenever in his presence, and seemed disposed to shun him. Mrs. Vess was friendly — almost too friendly he thought. Then there were still more rumors; worse still, there seemed to be no end to them. Stewart was a home wrecker. He had been chased out of Kentucky at the point of a gun by the father of a girl he had ruined.

Vess' "confusion" was explained in part a few days later. A report had reached the Purchase that Stewart had left for that region a few days after his arrival in Madison County. When he had failed to show up Vess and Clanton at once concluded him dead. Apparently Vess had not questioned the report of his death, for when Stewart arrived he had already taken steps for administering his estate. He had forged a claim against him equaling in amount the value of his property, when as a matter of fact he was indebted to Stewart. He was embrarrassed as well as surprised when he saw Stewart ride up. He did not know what to make of the situation.

Stewart had never looked upon Vess or his wife as worthy of the character which Clanton had given them. But houses, and especially boarding places, were scarce at that time in the Purchase. He had always considered Vess a lazy, shiftless fellow, but harmless. Stewart passed the claim matter off as gracefully as possible. Just as soon as an opportunity offered he would change his boarding place. At present he knew of no other. After much deliberation Stewart mentioned the matter of the claim to Clanton, asking if Vess had ever discussed it with him. Clanton replied that "he had, but that he was drunk, and he had attributed it all to that." Maybe Vess' drinking was responsible for his action and his enmity was not so marked as he had thought. Stewart wanted to believe that.

But a few days later he was to have his suspicions heightened all over again. During the day he had been examining and taking the numbers of unappropriated lands. It was late when he returned home. Vess and his wife had already eaten, but Mrs. Vess had kept his supper waiting. She prepared him a cup of warm coffee to drink with his cold meal.

He sipped the cup of warm coffee, and was in the act of accepting Mrs. Vess' offer of a second when he suddenly felt sick. He rose from the table vomiting violently. His vomiting, continued by repeated draughts of warm water, gave him some relief from the terrible sickness at his stomach. Each spell of vomiting was followed by great debility, accompanied with spasmodic symptoms. Stewart's strength, it seemed, would give way entirely. He was stunned. Mrs. Vess flirted about as one who wanted to do everything, but she did nothing. She was acting queerly. Then the thought struck Stewart: the cup had been poisoned; they had meant to get him out of the way in that manner; he grew still weaker at the thought of it. But after a while he gained some strength. He went off to bed, trembling.

Next day Stewart received another terrible fright. He had almost as narrow an escape as that of the night before. He was returning home in the afternoon, from the examination of a tract of land in a neighboring settlement, when a man rode up from his rear and fell in company with him, armed with a pair of holsters and a large Buoyer knife. Stewart's suspicion, already on edge, was kindled by the strangers' equipments. He felt uneasy. Contrary to custom, he had gone off that day unarmed. The man bore the countenance of a ruffian. If the man should be one of Murrell's tribe "he saw his only safety in cautious and well managed dissimulation." Stewart had become skeptical of everyone now.

The traveler rode up alongside him. They greeted each other after the fashion of travelers. The holstered man asked directions about roads and the next town. Stewart answered as an accomodating stranger. The man kept asking questions, as strangers will. Did he have any acquaintances in the country about Troy? Did he know a family of Glens? Stewart felt his body quiver in the saddle. The Glens were on his list of clansmen. His hunch had been correct.

"Are you acquainted with a man in this country by the name of Virgil Stewart?" the stranger asked.

"Yes," said Stewart coolly, "about as well as I care to know all such fellows."

"What! You don't like him, sir!"

"I have seen people I liked as well."

The man was interested. He reined his horse over closer, and shifted himself in the saddle so as to face Stewart easily. "Have you any particular objections to this fellow Stewart?"

"Oh! Yes. Many." Stewart said, and stopped, as if the subject was too distastefull to talk about.

The man's oily face wrinkled. He looked at Stewart slyly. "'If you don't mind I should like to hear what your objections are."

"Why," said Stewart somewhat reluctantly. "He's too smart. Interferes with things that don't concern him."

And then, without making his movements conspicuous, the man carefully gave the sign of the clan. Stewart answered it. The rider's eyes beamed.

"Oh," he laughed, "so you are up to it, eh?"

The men shook hands as two brothers of a fraternity. The slick face of the stranger carried a cold smile. "I'm glad to see you, sir," he said. "What is your name?"

"I have several names," Stewart said smoothly; "but whenever I wish to be very smart, or successful in speculation and trade, I go by the name of Tom Goodwin. I see you are a master of mystic signs. What is your name, sir?"

It was George Aker; and he announced with an oath that he was on a mission from "our council to stop the wind of Stewart."

Once Aker was started he raved on, telling what the clan would do to that damn meddling Stewart. If he could just catch sight of him! He told how the clan had met and agreed upon a plan to "destroy the rascal and restore the character to those whom he had betrayed. . . . But we've got him in a close box," Aker said winking. "He is living with his enemies, and the friends of some of the men he has slandered. We will give him hell before we quit him!" He told how the clansmen were planning to get Murrell out of prison and keep him off until court set, and in the meantime get a charge against Stewart that would disgrace him. When the session of court opened Murrell would appear for trial, thereby convincing the people that he was innocent of the charge. And should Stewart appear "we will prove him one of the greatest rascals that live." Murrell would be acquitted, and the character of those who had been defamed would be restored. "But we never intend for Stewart to live till the trial. . . . We will kill him and disgrace him, too."

Stewart held a bold face. He told Aker that he had been waiting "for a good opportunity," that he had managed to get acquainted with Stewart, had had some fair chances, but had been waiting for a better one. "I have been waiting to get him off alone."

Yes, the matter was supposed to have been attended to before now. He didn't know why it had not been done. And then Aker told Stewart something that confirmed his suspicion about Vess.

"We have it all fixed. The fellow with whom he lives is a good friend to some of our clan. . . . We sent one fellow before, who engaged the old man and his wife to poison him for a hundred dollars. But for some cause they have not done it."

The clan had become impatient; they had made up two hundred dollars and sent Aker to "dispatch the traitor." He said that Clanton was a "big bug" in the clan. The clan had promised to give him a thousand dollars to raise

a charge against Stewart. The men had done business together, and therefore it would be easy for Clanton to make
a plausible accusation. He would charge Stewart with
embezzling funds from his store while he was away on business, and also charge that he had passed counterfeit. But
Clanton would do nothing until Stewart was dead. They
had always been very good friends and "he wants no investigation by the young Tartar."

Clanton! Of all people whom Stewart felt that he could
trust it was Clanton. That was the worst blow of all.
Aker raved on, fuming with hatred, and boasting of what
he would do. If Aker did not get a chance at Stewart before leaving the Purchase, "we intend to bring men from
Arkansas with an accusation against him for passing
counterfeit money." They would be officers of the law to
whom respectable citizens of Arkansas had made com-
plaints. "And when we get him back into the Mississippi
swamp we will give him hell; we will give him something
to do beside acting the spy. We will speechify him next
time."

If they could kill Stewart, many people would appear
to make charges. It was easy enough to say that one had
been handed counterfeit money without fear of a perjury
charge if the man who had passed it was safely silenced
with a bullet. Aker smiled broadly. "And this is a good
one," and he nudged Stewart's leg. "Vess will charge adult-
ery against his wife."

The men's horses had slowed to a poking, stiff walk.
They were nearing the settlement. Stewart felt uneasy.
It would never do for some of his acquaintances to see him
now.

They were preparing to separate. Aker made a
strange proposition. He offered him half of his two hundred if he would kill Stewart. Perhaps Goodwin was better

acquainted than he. The hundred dollars might offer sufficient encouragement to get the job over now. . . . "And
that is not all you will get if you are successful in stopping
that villain's wind." Stewart hesitated. There the man
was poking a hundred dollars at him to destroy his own
life. He took the money. "If you can get no other chance,
shoot him as he sits by the fire." Then they would make
their escape into Arkansas. "We can do nothing until he
is dead," Aker explained.

Aker said he would spend the night at the Glen's.
Goodwin could meet him there in the morning after the
job was done. But Stewart suggested that they meet "on
the path which leads from Glen's to Commerce, at a pile
of house-logs." Stewart warned him that it would be better not to tell Glen or any person about what was going on.
The two were enough to know it. Aker agreed. The men
shook hands, and in true fraternal fashion gave the mystic sign of the clan and parted.

Now that Clanton had been revealed as his enemy
Stewart did not know whom he could trust. There was
only one acquaintance in the neighborhood, whom he
thought of at the moment, whom he felt he might trust,
George N. Saunders; and he was a close friend of Clanton.

He dared not eat with the Vess'. He ate supper with
his friend Saunders, and then went to the Vess place for
the night. He feared even to tell Saunders what had happened.

Stewart had planned to take a friend with him to
meet Aker next morning as a pretended accomplice. But
on second thought he feared to risk the confidence of anyone. He could not be sure that he had a friend in the entire
community. So early next morning Stewart was on the
road alone, gun in hand, making the best of his way to
the pile of house-logs. He could hear his heart pounding

heavily. He did not know what the next minute might bring.

When he arrived at the place Aker was not there. Stewart drew up in the edge of the woods and waited tensely, his eyes strained every moment watching for the man. An hour passed, and no one showed up. Then another hour. Stewart kept his tryst alone. Doubtless the would-be killer had learned of his blunder, and had gone back to the Arkansas swamps without his man, and also minus a hundred dollars of his blood money.

Just what Stewart's plans were, were never revealed. Whether he intended to arrest the man, or to lead him on for more information concerning the plots against him, or to kill him were never expressed. If the clansman had realized his position too dangerous to carry out his plans, certainly Stewart's position was ten times worse. And Stewart realized it.

Stewart was hurriedly arranging his affairs to leave when startling news reached the Purchase, and the alarm spread: Murrell had broken jail and escaped.

Now with Murrell out of jail, to confer with his clansmen, to plan his defence with a free hand, there was little safety for Stewart. He made Saunders agent for his property, and with all haste set out for Lexington, Kentucky, where he planned to hide out and publish Murrell's confessions. He did not let his route or destination be known.

He slipped in to pay the Hennings a visit on the way and to find out something of how affairs were going in those parts. He found the same abuse of his character there as elsewhere.

A few days of secret rest, and Stewart set out again for Lexington.

Near the end of his first day's travel he was startled

by the pounding of hoofs behind him. He was on a long stretch in the road; he could not recognize the man in the distance. His first impulse was to take to the woods for shelter. He could not know how many men might be pursuing him. But how did the clansmen know where he was? He had told no one except the Hennings. The rider was going fast. He was spurring his horse every jump. Stewart drew his gun quickly. He had decided to make a stand. The rider hailed him, spurred his horse into a faster gait. He came galloping on until he rode up even with Stewart, his horse blowing, and in a lather of sweat.

Stewart recognized the horseman. He was one of Parson Henning's sons. Stewart lowered his gun with relief. "He has come to warn me that the clan is after me," Stewart thought suddenly. But the youngster told a different story, and it was the best news Stewart had heard in months. Murrell had been recaptured.

Somewhere down near Florence, Alabama, he had been recognized in a tavern. He had been traveling concealed in a wagon of grain, and had stepped out to eat. A few miles further on down the road officers took charge of him.

Now that Murrell had been recaptured Stewart was needed to testify at the trial, for he was the only witness in that part of the state.

Stewart turned back.

They brought Murrell back to Jackson, raging, cursing, telling what would happen to that damn hypocrite Stewart. He had friends, and this meddling rascal would pay for all his trouble.

They locked him again in the county jail. This time they watched him more closely. Visitors were admitted only under the closest observation.

Trial was set for July.

CHAPTER XV.

TRIAL

DURING the last days of July, 1834, John A. Murrell was brought to trial at the Circuit Court which sat at Jackson in Madison County. People had swarmed in from everywhere. The mystery and great publicity that had been given the case had created anxiety and excitement. It had been rumored that the clan would rush the court room and take Murrell away. Stewart had been threatened anew that if he attempted to give his evidence he would be shot in the act. Many came through pure curiosity. Others came prepared for action.

The court room was packed to overflowing when Murrell was escorted in. Officers had to wedge an opening through the swarming mob of curious spectators that the defendant might have room to walk. Necks were stretching to get a glimpse of this strange man. Murrell held the poise for which he was noted. His dignity was impressive. He smiled at a few friends he recognized in the audience. He wanted the people to believe that he was taking the whole thing lightly.

Perhaps Murrell did have considerable confidence in his support. He had three of the best lawyers that could be secured. Chief of the defence counsel was the distinguished Milton Brown, the man who was later to introduce

the bill in Congress by which Texas was annexed to the
United States. To assist him were Colonel John Read of
Jackson and Mr. Harris of Brownsville.

Stewart was the only important witness for the State.
Would Stewart's story be accepted? Murrell's fate hung
upon the answer to that question.

Stewart was called and sworn. Part of the time he
read from the notes he had made of the conversation with
Murrell on that strange ride into Arkansas. At other
times he looked up from his manuscript and in narrative
fashion told the jury of Murrell's confessions. He commenced by giving a narrative of his adventure and developing all the circumstances and occurrences which led to his
introduction to Murrell. He related how Murrell had
spoken in the third person of the two brothers, of the
clever feats they had accomplished, and later how he had
heard from the prisoner accounts of his horrible deeds
along the Mississippi, his evangelical campaigns, his extensive negro stealing. He read from his manuscript in
direct quotations, often in the familiar language of Murrell. Much of it apparently had no direct bearing upon the
case of negro stealing for which the defendant was charged.
But Judge Haskell sustained no objections. And Stewart
would not stop until the last word was read.

A muffled, confused roar went over the court room
when Stewart told of the planned negro rebellion. It was
too ridiculous for many to believe. There were a few his-
ses and sneers. Judge Haskell pounded heavily with the
gavel before the room was again brought to silence.

When the list of the clansmen was read the room went
into confusion. There were guffaws and hoots and cheers
by partisans and enemies of the clan. Stewart was forced
to stop a number of times before the list was finished. It

was all the judge could do for a while to keep a semblance of order.

It was noon of the second day before Stewart completed his testimony. The court adjourned for dinner.

When Stewart stepped down from the witness stand the case was practically over except for the character witnesses. The defence found itself distressingly short of witnesses. If Stewart had not possessed a list of the clansmen the case might have turned out differently. Murrell might have proven anything with his friends, and doubtless would have. Now they were afraid to appear in court lest they should be known and apprehended. The men whom Murrell had named in his circular who stated that they had seen Stewart and Murrell together at Jehu Barney's place and who had sworn "in due form of law" that they had heard Stewart say that he was to get five hundred dollars for effecting Murrell's conviction never appeared to testify. Clanton, who of late had issued such slanders at Stewart, never came closer than the Choctaw Purchase. No one knew just who was included on the list. Murrell himself did not remember. It was an embarrassing situation for Murrell. Turning this list over to Stewart was his worst blunder.

In the afternoon character witnesses, who had been summoned, took the stand to vouch for Stewart's honesty.

Then came the defense's turn. A certain Reuben M'-Vey was produced as a witness to prove that the Reverend Henning had hired Stewart to detect the defendant, and that he had a personal interest in a conviction. It might have looked bad for Stewart had not the prosecuting attorneys tangled the witness. Soon he was stammering and blurting out incoherent contradictions. Long before the trial was over it was brought before the court that Stewart would not even receive a handsome suit of clothes which

Parson Henning wished to purchase for him, as a remuneration for his time and labor in pursuit of the negroes. It was further called to the attention of the court that M'Vey had for some time entertained a deep hatred toward Stewart because Stewart had refused to associate with him, not regarding him as a gentleman.

Attorney Brown could not be discouraged. He raved forth with all his oratory and wit. It was a famous as well as important case, and Brown was known as a hard-hitting, ambitious lawyer. He was determined to free his client at any effort. His questions in the cross-examination were cutting and bitter and full of insinuations. His wit caused the court room to roar with laughter. He questioned Stewart about the pretty Arkansas girls of which he and Murrell had talked. He was determined to make the testimony appear a ridiculous farce, and the witness a vain, sensational story teller who was out for profit.

Addressing the jury, Brown reached his height. It seemed that the man was carried away with his own self. He spoke with the flowery, crisp oratory for which he was later noted. He appealed to the jurors' sense of honor. Stewart had admitted that through deceit he had won Murrell's confidence, had been made a member of the clan, he had taken an oath; and he had betrayed all. He spoke on patriotism in flaming words; a man who would betray a fraternal brother and break a binding oath would betray his country. He made Biblical references in dramatic solemnity; he ridiculed the idea of conspiracy until the very suggestion became funny. The idea of prominent men being connected with such a clan as Stewart spoke of was still more childish and silly. He aired all the gossip that had circulated against Stewart. "Who could testify to this man's private life for any period of time?" he shouted.

Fortunately for Stewart, his enemies were afraid to

show their faces, or it would perhaps have been his immediate ruin.

Attorneys Read and Harris let Brown do most of the talking. He seemed to be outdoing himself that day. Near the end of the afternoon Brown made one last great outburst of oratory in an appeal for justice, reminded his jurors that it was better that ten guilty men should go free than that one innocent one should suffer for a crime that he had never committed. He referred also in conclusion to the rumors about Stewart that "had come from Georgia."

Then he sat down. The judge charged the jury, and the twelve men who held Murrell's fate in their hands marched out to make their decision.

It had begun to grow dark. Long shadows were fading in the court room. An eager crowd waited. Prosecuting attorney General Alexander B. Bradford, and his assistant, Major A. L. Martin waited anxiously. Brown sat with his associates near-by mopping the perspiration from his face nervously. A strained silence hung over the court room. Both partisans and enemies of Murrell feared the consequence of the verdict. It was the most important trial that Jackson had ever witnessed.

Thirty minutes after Judge Haskell had completed his charge, the jury marched back into the court room. Grim-faced men leaned forward eagerly. A death silence went over the court room. And then the verdict was read. . . . Murrell was pronounced guilty of negro stealing, as charged.

Judge Haskell commanded the prisoner to rise and hear his sentence. He rose slowly, as if in a daze. He was sentenced to the state penitentiary for a term of ten years at hard labor. Then his face reddened with rage. But he said nothing, nor made any outward gesture. His muscles seemed drawn as if poisoned by the bitterness of his own rage. He just stood there motionless and stiff until the guards came and marched him off to his jail cell.

Stewart was much incensed by Brown's actions in court. He prepared to give him the thrashing of his life as soon as he could catch him on the streets. Older men, however, prevailed upon Stewart not to do so; and the controversy was taken up verbally through various indirect channels. It became intensely bitter, and articles were exchanged in the newspapers. Brown's influence had done much to make the slanderous charge against Stewart appear credible. Stewart was yet struggling to save his name. Perhaps if he had been less sensitive the charges would have been forgotten sooner, and he would have subjected himself to less embarrassment. But he worked untiringly to completely exonerate his name. He collected affidavits from all parts of the country to verify his actions and to attest to his character. Some were requested by Stewart. Many were sent to him voluntarily. They came chiefly from officials, and people prominent in society and business, as well as from those who had occasion to know something directly of his work in detecting Murrell. There were the affidavits of John Champion and Matthew Erwin, at whose homes Stewart and Murrell had visited on their route to Arkansas; one signed by Orville Shelby, and also from the five guards who took Murrell in Madison County; a long list from Holmes County in the state of Mississippi testifying to Stewart's conduct and standing in the Purchase. Then there were sworn statements concerning the character witnesses who appeared in behalf of the defendant, as well as affidavits regarding characters who issued slander against Stewart.

The prosecuting attorney, Alexander B. Bradford
wrote to Stewart:

"Jackson, Tennessee, October 10th, 1835
"Mr. Virgil A. Stewart:—

"Sir—At your request, and in justice to you and other
persons concerned in the trial and conviction of John A.
Murrell, late of Madison County, Tennessee, for the crime
of negro-stealing, I deem it my duty to make the following
statement.

"At the July term of the Circuit Court of said county,
I indicted the said John A. Murrell for the crime above
described, at which time he was tried, convicted, and sentenced to be confined in the penitentiary for ten years;
I have prosecuted the pleas of the state for many years,
during all which time I have never known any prisoner
to have a fairer or more impartial trial than Murrell had
on this occasion. He was defended by several counsel,
and that, too, with zeal and ability; and they were allowed
by the court every latitude usual in such cases; and the
jury who passed upon his case stand as high for honesty
and intelligence as any men in the county.

"In relation to yourself I have to say, that Murrell
was convicted mainly upon your testimony, the facts of
which were lengthy and complicated; that you underwent
a most rigid cross-examination, and I have no hesitation
in saying that I never heard any man sustain himself better. Your character was attacked directly in the defense,
yet your veracity was sustained by some of our most worthy
citizens, among whom were Colonel Thomas Loftin, of
this county (Madison), and Alexander Patton, Esquire,
of this place. Indeed, the ample testimony borne on your
good character was highly creditable. Until the trial of
Murrell, you were to me an entire stranger; still the impression made upon me by you was favorable, and, as an

officer of the government, I was satisfied at the time that
he was rightfully and legally convicted of the crime of
negro-stealing, on your evidence, and I have yet no reason
to doubt it; and, moreover, the verdict of the jury, as I
believe, met with the general sanction of those who witnessed the trial.

"Given under my hand, at Jackson, the date above.

Alexander B. Bradford

Solicitor General of the 14th District
in the State of Tennessee."

Stewart was a sensative soul who spared no energy in
an effort to save his good name. But his days of peace
were gone.

A motion for a new trial was filed. But the motion
was promptly overruled. A few days later Murrell was
carried away under heavy guard to the state penitentiary
at Nashville. He began his term on August 17, 1834.

Many people in Nashville came for a look at this
strange character. Among others was a noted phrenologist, O. S. Fowler. He asked the authorities' permission
to make a phrenological reading of Murrell's head. The
request was granted. The report of his findings was no
surprise: "Energy, Acquisitiveness were fully developed;
Secretiveness, quite large; Self-Esteem, large and active;
Adhesiveness, slight." The phrenologist said: "He has
natural Ability, if it had been rightly called out and directed, for a superior Scholar, scientific man, a lawyer, or
a Statesman."

A contemporary historian wrote of Murrell's conviction: "Murrell's conviction in 1834 acted as a great clari-
fication to the atmosphere. It discouraged the marauder
class and it gave heart to the citizens. So strong had the

clan been that no one was willing to run the risk of needlessly offending them."

With Murrell safely behind the bars of the state prison the Valley breathed easier now. People believed that Murrell's conviction was the end of the terrible clan, and that organized crime along the Mississippi was over. But they were wrong.

CHAPTER XVI

AFTER THE TRIAL

ONCE Murrell was lodged behind the iron bars of the State penitentiary his spirit fell. Nothing more was heard of his clever letter-writing, or of brilliant messages to his clansmen. Seemingly they had deserted him. His life's ambition had slipped away from him by a few short months. The small, crowded prison must have cramped the very soul of this wild adventurer who for years had roamed the country and known no restraint.

At the time of his confinement there were twenty-two vocations listed as giving employment to the convicts in the Tennessee State penitentiary. Those occupations which gave employment to the greatest number of men were listed as: "harness makers, blacksmiths, shoemakers, carpenter shop workers, hatters." There were also wagon makers, mattress makers, wool carders, makers of spinning wheels, painters, cooks and others. Forty-five of the prisoners, at the time the list was made, were employed preparing stones for the new capitol building. The list did not give the names of the men employed in the various vocations. So it is not known at what occupation Murrell worked. But strange stories drifted out from behind the stone walls as prisoners from time to time were released into the free world again. They told of this mysterious Murrell pouring over his Bible at night. He talked about being a great preacher some day. It was said also that he kept an old law book in his cell and that he read from it often. The man liked to read, and he never tired of parading his learning.

During the year 1834 fifty entrants were registered at the Tennessee penitentiary, including Murrell. They were an interesting assortment of associates. They were listed: murder 2nd degree 1, manslaughter 4, stabbing 1, assault to kill 1, burglary 2, *negro stealing* 2, receiving stolen goods 1, incest 1, forgery 4, counterfeiting 6, grand larceny 6, petit larceny 16, horse-stealing 5.

The penitentiary was small and over-crowded. The area within the prison walls was about 330 square feet. And much of this space was occupied by buildings. Within this small space were also the penthouses for the use of the inmates, the pits to which could be sunk only a few feet in consequence of the rocks lying near the surface. It was a pale, sickly herd of despondent creatures that occupied this place. A small, dirty hospital was always crowded to capacity. The death rate at the time was 5%. Only the hardiest could live many years here.

Murrell's arrest and conviction did not break up the clan. It might have been supposed that after the leader was caught and imprisoned, the conspiracy would have ended. But it was not so. The great outlaw king had embittered the clansmen with a poison that kept their passions on edge. They had worked too long and risked too much for their cherished plans to go crumbling to nothing. Murrell had said it could be done. Blindly they believed him. The conspiracy story had played no official part in the conviction. Milton Brown had made the plot appear ridiculous. The local paper at Jackson reported that Stewart "made too much effort at display" on the witness stand. It was difficult for Murrell's worst enemies to believe that such a conspiracy was under way. It was impossible!

Once Murrell was out of the way, citizens in the Valley began once more to talk of other subjects. If they had been frightened by Stewart's story, they felt safe now that the chief of the bandits was lodged securely behind stone walls. Even if there was something to the story, nobody except Murrell could execute such a mad scheme!

The outlaws of the Valley were determined to die hard. Back in the canebrakes and swamps, in the filthy taverns of the river towns, the clansmen met and discussed their plans. Without their leader they blundered along, arguing and fighting among themselves. But withall they were a determined bunch.

They made one sensible move, however. The leaders changed the date of the rebellion from Christmas to the Fourth of July before. If there were those who really believed the rebellion story, they would be caught off guard; and by setting an earlier date, they would give the upper world less time to investigate. And so the Fourth of July, 1835, was set as the date of the uprising of the negroes of the South.

The man who had most to worry about was Virgil A. Stewart. He remained in Madison County for a while after the trial, closely guarded by his friends, sleeping always with barred windows, never venturing out unless heavily armed. Every move that Stewart made was carefully watched by the clan. Private agents of the organization were sent to him in the guise of friends to represent to him the dangerous position in which he would place himself by publishing his notes. It was also suggested to him the possibility that the clan might be willing to advance a large amount of money to insure his secrecy. When outright bribery failed, mysterious, and open threats came.

Stewart had two purposes in making a publication— as a vindication, and as a warning to the slave states of the South. The less the people believed in him, the less they believed in the possibility of a conspiracy.

Enemies continued to stir the gossip that had proven so embarrassing: He was a libertine, a home-wrecker, a counterfeiter, a roving vagabond. There seemed to be no let up to it.

Stewart realized the insecurity of his position. If he should be killed there would no one to vindicate his character, and there would be no further warning for the South. On the twenty-eighth of September Stewart slipped quietly out of Madison County bound for Lexington, Kentucky, where he planned to arrange his notes and publish his story. He took an indirect route and avoided the well-known roads.

On the night of the 29th he put up at a small, country tavern where he thought he should be most likely to pass the night without observation. He had hardly completed his arrangements for lodging when four men pushed into the tavern and made known their intention of passing the night. They forced conversation with Stewart. They asked about roads, distances, the best place to cross the Tennessee River. What course was he taking through Tennessee, what ferry would he use, what direction then? They were all natural questions that might arise during any conversation among travelers. But they made the reserved Stewart uncomfortable. By his answers he indicated that he had business in the neighborhood which would detain him for several days. Then he excused himself as promptly as possible.

By daybreak the next morning the four strangers had left the tavern. An hour or so later Stewart departed over the same road.

Stewart rode with a nervous sense of apprehension. He could not get the thought of the four men off his mind. Early in the afternoon he put up at the home of a Mr. Gilbert. It was the morning of October 2 before he felt safe to travel again.

Stewart changed his course slightly. He planned now to cross the Tennessee at Patton's Ferry and pursue his journey through Columbia in Murry County, and thence to Lexington, Kentucky, by way of Nashville. It was a wild, desolate, unsettled region that lay between Jackson and Patton's Ferry. Tall trees and thick undergrowth made high, weird walls that hedged the narrow wilderness road for miles and miles. There were no sounds to break the wilderness silence except the wild life of the vast forest.

Some eight or ten miles from Patton's Ferry Stewart was startled by the sudden appearance of three armed men, who stepped from behind trees and ordered him to dismount. It suddenly flashed to Stewart's mind that he had inquired of the tavern keeper the nearest road to Patton's Ferry. He recognized one of the men as one of the four who had passed the night at the tavern.

The leader of the band stood to Stewart's right "about two rods distance" armed with a large fowling piece. His companion on the left held a long rifle. The third member of the gang placed himself back against a tree, immediately in front of Stewart's horse. He was armed with a heavy barreled pistol. The leader drew closer and demanded if he intended to dismount or not. Stewart replied, "No." The man leveled his piece. Stewart, who always kept his pistol convenient, drew quickly and fired in the man's face before he had time to suspect such an event. The ball entered his forehead. He dropped, apparently lifeless. As he fell his gun went off, passing harmlessly under the belly of Stewart's horse. At this turn of events the assailant on his left fired, and missed, and for a moment there was only one man to contend with, the one in front, who at that moment charged upon him. He made the mistake of coming too close, knowing now that Stewart's piece was not loaded. For as he rushed close on to Stewart, Stewart threw his pistol with all force into his face striking him over the eye. He was stunned for the moment. Stewart then stuck spurs to his horse and charged into the man with a long knife which he had drawn. But as he bent over to strike his assailant he received a severe blow across his breast from the heavy rifle in the hands of the attacker on the left. He was stunned for a moment, and before he could regain his natural position in the saddle another blow pounded upon the back of his head and neck, jarring his entire body. The blow sent him bouncing forward upon his horse's neck. He realized that the last blow was serious; and as soon as he could regain his saddle he put spurs to his horse and dashed into the thick woods with all speed. As he darted off a buckshot struck him in the arm. But it did no serious injury.

Stewart got away; delirious, swaying crazily. He rode with all speed, the undergrowth tearing his flesh. Long before he felt the safety of it, he was forced to stop. He felt that he might lose his senses any minute. He tumbled off his horse, tied him, and half blinded, crawled off into a grove of thick undergrowth.

Rest brought him no ease. Night came on and he
was numb and delirious; he frequently found himself
crawling through the brush and thicket as if under the
influence of a horrible dream. Towards daybreak he got
a moment's rest; but he awoke in almost unbearable pain.
His neck was swollen, and his body was burning with
fever; his wounded arm was stiff and sore, and his whole
frame was racked with misery. It dawned upon Stewart's
befuddled mind that the clansmen would never let him
live so long as one could lay an eye on him. He could
never be safe in this country—certainly not after his disclosures were in print. He was not nearly as safe as the
outlaws who hunted him. He was a hunted man who did
not know his own enemies. To continue his journey on
to Lexington would mean almost certain death; to return
to Madison County promised no better. In this desperate
position Stewart determined to leave America.

In the late afternoon he pulled himself upon his horse
and started in a southerly direction, only vaguely knowing where his course might lead. He wanted to go into
Mississippi, from there to Mobile. From Mobile he would
go to some part of Europe for a few years.

He rode until near midnight, when he came to a large
creek. He could find no way to cross the stream. He
fell down on the ground for a few hours' rest. Next morning he awoke cold and damp and with a violent cold. He
pushed on, half-conscious, until near noon of the 4th before he could get food for himself and his horse; he feared
to present himself in prominent places.

On the edge of the Chickasaw Nation, Stewart took
lodging with an old Indian until his fever abated. Then
he set out again southward, and fell in with a party of
ladies and gentlemen, in whose company he decided to
travel to some port on the Mississippi. From there he

would catch a boat to New Orleans. But he soon found it impossible to ride faster than a walk; he gradually fell behind; he was suffering from torturing pains; and a burning fever seemed that it would consume him. He grew fainter and fainter until he could no longer support himself. Then he came falling senseless to the ground.

A wagoner passing by stopped and dragged him out of the road. In this state he was found by a friend who was traveling down to Memphis, a fellow by the name of Augustus Q. Walton.

Walton carried Stewart to a neighboring farmhouse. Stewart was trying to tell him something; he talked of attacks, grave dangers, and secrecy, but it was all a confusing babble. It was late the next afternoon before he began to talk sense. He told Walton that he had to leave the country with all haste—and his work had not been completed. He did not know in what direction to turn. Walton had been helpful in caring for him. He said that he wished that he might do more.

Through this suggestion came a part solution of Stewart's problem. He turned his notes over to Walton upon his promise to superintend their publication. He handed him some money. He wanted nothing to prevent publication. Walton promised to meet Stewart in Natchez as soon as affairs would permit.

Stewart was more hopeful now. He felt that his disclosures would be published whether he lived or not. He went on to Natchez and remained there under an assumed name until he was somewhat recovered, and leaving a letter for his friend, he left Natchez for St. Francisville. Here he spent his time writing out more notes which he wished to give Walton.

On November 10 Walton arrived at St. Francisville, and the two men set out for New Orleans. But when they reached New Orleans Stewart's health had become so bad that his friend persuaded him not to attempt to go to Europe.

There was only one way to turn now—up the river. Under an assumed name, and avoiding all unnecessary exposure, Stewart made his way quietly up the river with Walton.

They spent the winter in Cincinnati.

Although Stewart had been too ill to give the manuscript much attention it was completed by spring and ready for the public. The product was a pulp paper volume of eighty-four pages. It bore a price mark of twenty-five cents, and contined six illustrations, artificial and typical of the day. Walton's name appeared as that of the author.

The long title given the book was typical of the day: *A History of the Detection, Conviction, Life and Designs of John A. Murrell The Great Western Land Pirate together with his System of Villainy and Plan of Executing a Negro Rebellion, Also a Catalogue of the Names of Four Hundred and Fifty-Five of his Mystic Clan Fellows and Followers and a Statement of their efforts for the destruction of Virgil A. Stewart the young man who detected him to which is added a Biographical Sketch of Virgil A. Stewart.* The last statement in the volume read: "Mr. Stewart is recovering his health and mind, both of which have been greatly injured."

The pamphlet was promptly distributed throughout the South. The clansmen had enjoyed a rest while Stewart was hid out in Cincinnati. They were content to let his name be forgotten. Perhaps they thought he had been frightened out of the country for good; at least he had been frightened into secrecy. They went into a rage when their eyes fell upon the pamphlet and they found that the book was scattered all over the country. There was the whole bloody story; an account of the detection, Stewart's conversations with Murrell, his mysterious experiences at clan headquarters, the plot against the slave holders, and worst of all a list of the clansmen! It was a puzzled South that read this strange book.

Again the clan went to work. They could not find Stewart, for he never dared show himself except in disguise. But again they started their slander against him. They even brought forth a counter pamphlet impeaching his honor. To Stewart's great surprise George N. Saunders had joined with the others against him. The pamphlet contained sworn statements concerning Stewart's villainy. He had beat his debts, he had swindled his neighbors, Clanton charged that Stewart had stolen his household furnishings while he was away from home. It seemed that the clan was trying to outdo Stewart at pamphlet writing.

The clan used another system of defense. Stewart's little book was eagerly purchased, presumably by members of the clan, and within a few months after it first appeared, it was out of print, and a copy could not be bought for fifty dollars.

The pamphlet was hardly a success either as a warning or a vindication. This horrible scheme of wholesale murder by the negroes was too mad a scheme ever to become a reality! In the main it only added to discredit Stewart's truthfulness. People believed that Murrell headed a clan, which had been guilty of almost every known crime. They had known enough of his meanness first hand to believe almost anything about him. But now that Murrell was in prison people wanted to forget about it.

And so it was left to the clan itself to reveal its purpose.

CHAPTER XVII

THE SOUTH WAKES UP

NEAR the end of June, 1835, an alarming rumor spread out from the little community of Beatie's Bluff in Madison County, Mississippi. It was not long before the entire county was in a turmoil.

There had been a few suspicious acts observed among the colored population, and some vague fears had been aroused. But in spite of all the talk about Murrell and Stewart, few people seemed to have taken the conspiracy matter seriously until a certain Mrs. Latham overheard a strange conversation between two of her slaves.

For some time Mrs. Latham had noticed in her house servants "a disposition to be insolent and disobedient," and occasionally they had used insulting and contemptuous language in her hearing. This deportment was very unusual; and when she found her negro girls in secret conversation when they should have been about their duties, she determined to watch their conduct more closely. She was not able to hear the entire conversation: "I wish to God it was all over and done with; I's tired of waiting on the white folks," one of the negresses was saying to the other; "I want to be my own mistress and clean my own house."

Soon after, she caught one of the same girls in secret conversation with a negro from one of the neighboring plantations. The girl was holding one of Mrs. Latham's grandchildren in her arms. From the low tones in which they talked she was not able to get all the conversation. However, she heard the negro nurse say: "But ain't it a pity to kill as pretty little baby as this? This is such a pretty child," she pleaded. But the visiting negro replied: "Gal, when the day comes you-all got to." They went on mumbling strange things about the white folk and killing people. Mrs. Latham could not understand well. She stepped away quietly, and sent for her son who was away in the fields.

Upon his arrival he had the negress brought before him. She was told that her entire conversation had been overheard; and now she must tell what it was all about. The girl, thinking all was overheard, without hesitation or punishment came out with what she knew. She said that the negro man had informed her that there was to be a rising of the black people soon, and that they intended killing all the white folk. When she had pleaded against killing the baby the black man had said that it would be doing them a service, as they would go to heaven and be rid of much trouble in this world.

Soon men were riding from plantation to plantation spreading the direful warning that plans were under way for an uprising of the blacks and a general massacre of the whites. Meetings were held in different parts of the country; patrols were organized and committees of viligance appointed.

On the 27th of June a large general meeting was held at Livingston, the county seat. Other suspicious acts had been observed. The men proceeded to organize in a manner that would insure the prompt action that the situation demanded. Resolutions were adopted, and committees of investigation was appointed.

On June 30th, the citizens met again at Livingston. The first additional bit of information that they were able to gather came in a very round-about way. William P. Johnson, a member of the committee of investigation, had instructed his driver, a negro in whom he had all confidence, to examine all the negroes on his plantation and see if they knew anything of the conspiracy. The driver had learned from an old negro, who was in the habit of hauling water from Livingston, that there was to be "a rising of the blacks soon, but did not know when; that he had learned it from a negro man named Peter belonging to Ruel Blake, who lived in Livingston." Johnson's driver had asked the old negro for some powder and shot, pretending that he wanted it to shoot the white people with when the uprising should take place. The old negro had replied that he had none, but could get some from Ruel Blake's boy, Peter. Peter had helped unload some kegs at a store belonging to William M. Ryce, and had learned at the time that they contained powder. Peter had told of his plans to break into the store and steal some of the kegs of powder.

It was a scattered, complicated story, but the committee went to work on it. The old negro was immediately sent for. He was asked to tell the investigating committee what he had told Johnson's driver the evening before. He denied ever having had any conversation with the driver. He would confess nothing.

But a few licks from a whip loosened his tongue, and

he came out with all he had told Johnson's negro. He did
not know what particular day was fixed for the insurrection. Peter had told him he would let him know in a few
days.

Peter had already been sent for. He was pushed before the committee and questioned about the insurrection.
He just stood there and said nothing. He was ordered to
be whipped by the committee. But he stubbornly refused
to confess anything, alleging all the time, that if they
wanted to know what his master had told him they would
never learn. He said he had promised that he would never
tell it. This was strange talk; but it was overlooked at
the time.

It was the general impression at this time that the
uprising would take place on the night of July 4, for on
this day the negroes were allowed a holiday and were allowed to assemble from the different plantations.

The boy who was overheard by Mrs. Latham at
Beatie's Bluff had run off. The negroes examined by
the committee having implicated no white men as accomplices, it was the general impression that the conspiracy
was confined to the negroes of a few plantations. It was
agreed upon by common consent of the citizens assembled
in the various meetings, that as soon as the ringleaders in
the plot should be detected, they should immediately be
made examples and hanged. This would strike terror
among the rest.

Still men refused to believe the Murrell plot.

Meanwhile the citizens at Beatie's Bluff had not been
idle. One by one suspected slaves had been rounded up.
On the first day of July a meeting was held. The girls
from the Latham plantation were examined by a committee, and they stated again that the negroes intended rising

and slaying all the whites. A negro blacksmith, by the name of Joe, was brought before the examining committee. He acted surprised. He could not imagine what the men wanted. They told him that Sam, a fellow servant, had told of a conversation the two had had in the shop. The negro trembled. The men called for a rope and tied his hands. Then the negro pleaded that if they would not punish him he would tell them what they wanted to know, but that he himself had nothing to do with the business. He said that Sam had told him that the negroes were going to rise and kill all the whites on the Fourth, and that they had a number of white men at their head. Some of them Joe knew by name, others he knew only when he saw them.

White men! The plot was taking a deeper turn than the committee expected. Joe mentioned the following white men as actively engaged in the business: Ruel Blake, Doctors Cotton and Saunders, and many more, but could not call their names, but that he had seen several others. He aslo gave the names of several slaves as ring leaders in the business who were understood to be captains under these white men. He said that one of the captains, Weaver by name, belonged to his master. Another captain belonged to a Mr. Riley. His name was Russell. Both were preachers. He also implicated Sam as one of the captains.

Joe stated that the insurrection was to commence the Fourth of July; and the slaves of each plantation were to commence with axes, hoes, etc., and to massacre all the whites at home, and then were to make their way to Beatie's Bluff, where they were to break into the storehouses and get all the arms and ammunition that were in that place, and then proceed to Livingston, where they would obtain re-enforcements from the different plantations. From thence they were to go to Vernon and sack that place, recruiting as they went; and from there they were to proceed to Clinton. And by the time they took the last mentioned place they calculated they wuold be strong enough to bear down any and every opposition that could be brought against them from there to Natchez. After killing all the citizens in that place and plundering the banks, they were to retire to a place called the Devil's Punch Bowl. Here they were to make a stand, and no force that could be brought could take them.

The preachers, Russell and Weaver, were sent for. At first they denied everything; but they were told that their conversations had been overheard. Finally Russell came out with the whole matter. His statement was, in all particulars, precisely like the one made by Joe.

Next day the committee met at Beatie's Bluff and again took up their grim, gruesome work. More trembling blacks were pushed before the committee and confessions wrung from them; and hour by hour the plot took on a more serious appearance.

Among the other slaves brought in was one belonging to "Doctor" Saunders, by the name of Jim. His statement was very much like that of Joe's. He implicated, however, more white men by name, than Joe had done, as well as a few more slaves. There was a man present by the name of Donovan whom he pointed out as deeply implicated. He also told about a man by the name of Moss, and his sons, as being very friendly to the slaves; he said that to him they could sell all they could lay their hands on. He stated further that Moss had always furnished them with whiskey; and these bad white men always made Moss' house their home while in the neighborhood. But Jim did not know whether Moss intended taking any part in the insurrection or not.

Then he came out with something that chilled the blood

of white men. Jim stated that it was their intention to slay all the whites, except some of the most beautiful women. They had been told that each negro might keep one white woman for himself. He said that he had already picked out one for himself, and that he and his wife had already had a quarrel over it, when he told her of his intentions. He gave the names of Blake, Cotton, Saunders and Donovan as engaged in the plot.

A negro youth by the name of Bachus was examined, and he stated in substance what Jim had given. He added another white man to the list, a peddler, by the name of Silver, who was "making up money to buy arms." Bachus had given him six dollars for that purpose. But the peddler was never heard of again.

Along about sundown the negroes, Jim, Weaver, Russell, Sam, Bachus, and perhaps two or three others, were led out, hands tied behind, into a grove near Beatie's Bluff. They were all hanged.

The news of the trials and execution at Beatie's Bluff spread like a fire alarm in the stillness of the night. The conspiracy was not confined alone to a few daring and desperate negroes. The negroes were encouraged and backed by a desperate gang of whites, who apparently would stop at nothing. And no one knew the extent of their power and organization. It was the Murrell conspiracy unquestionably! People could not believe such a thing until it was actually revealed. They could not even conceive of the desperate Murrell being so bloodthirsty.

Such an emergency called for quick and concerted action. Calls were made on the governor for troops to aid in guard duty. At least the people knew now about what time the uprising was to commence. But the time was almost at hand, and the majority of the population being negroes made the situation alarming indeed. The

country was settled principally in large plantations, and
on many of them there was no white man other than an
overseer, as many of the planters were away at the North
at the time. In the neighborhood of Livingston and
Beatie's Bluff, where the scene of desolation was to commence, there were at least fifty negroes to one white
man. There was no organized militia in the country, and
no place of security as a retreat for the white families.
There was only one way. And that was for the citizens
to strike terror among the conspirators, to nip the plot in
the bud if possible.

There was no time to be lost. The call was sent out
for another general meeting at Livingston the next day.
And by daybreak of July 3rd, men were riding into Livingston from all directions. Not only Madison County but
the neighboring counties as well were represented.

A "Committee of Safety" comprising thirteen members invested by the citizens with the authority of punish-
ing all persons found guilty by them of aiding or exciting
the negro rebellion, was selected by the assembly. Resolutions were drawn up and were signed. The first paragraph
read as follows:

"Resolved, that a standing committee be by this meeting organized; that the said committee shall consist of
thirteen freeholders, that the committee shall have a regular secretary and chairman, that they do meet every day
at 9 o'clock, A. M., and sit until 4 o'clock P. M., that the
committee shall have power to appoint the captain of any
patrol company; to bring before them any person or persons, either white or black, and try in a summary manner
any person brought before them, with the power to hang
or whip, being always governed by the laws of the land
so far only as they shall be applicable to the case in ques-

tion otherwise to act as their discretion shall seem best for the benefit of the country, and for the protection of its citizens."

The committee, elected Doctor M. D. Mitchell chairman; William M. Boyce was made secretary. They adopted some rules to govern them in their examination of offenders. They determined to take no cognizance of any crime which was not directly connected with the contemplated insurrection; to examine all witnesses under oath; to punish no man without strong circumstantial evidence, in addition to the dying confessions of those previously executed, or such other evidence as should seem convincing to all of the guilt of the accused; to give every opportunity that the nature of the case would admit, to prove their good character, or any thing that would go to prove their innocence; and, in fact, to give them all the privileges allowed to criminals in courts of justice in similar cases, and to permit them to establish doubtful points by their own voluntary statements.

By ten o'clock the citizens had perfected their organization and the committee commenced its labours with the examination of the case of Joshua Cotton, which was already unofficially underway.

Cotton was a New Englander, who had lived in the state only about twelve months. Upon his arrival in Mississippi he had settled at the "old Indian Agency" in Hinds County, where he married soon after. From the Agency he moved to Livingston where he set up a shop and introduced himself as a "Steam Doctor."

It was said of him that he was in the constant habit of trading with negroes, and "would buy anything they would steal and bring to him." It was said also that he had left Memphis, soon after the conviction of Murrell, with a wife and child. Incidentally, when he arrived in Hinds County he was a very eligible single man. William Saunders had told that Cotton had made a proposition to him to take Cotton's second wife to Red River in Arkansas and leave her there, promising the wife that he would meet her there as soon as he should settle his affairs in Mississippi. At the same time he had confided to Saunders that his object was to abandon her. It was well known in Livingston that he showed a lack of feeling and affection for his wife. Cotton was known for his extensive riding about the country. He explained that he had a bunch of Spanish horses in the woods that he had to look about. It was known that on these trips he spent much time conversing with the negroes. When the negroes implicated Cotton it was none too hard for the citizens to believe the story, in view of his reputation.

Consequently Cotton had been arrested on the 1st, but nothing could be proved. Saunders, his partner, was about the only white man who had let out any definite information against him.

But Saunders was not to be found. He had left the country. Cotton had been turned loose.

But Saunders had one bad habit for a man engaged in a plot. He talked too much. On the road to Vickbsurg he fell in with a gentleman traveler. He broke the news of the trouble in Madison Country to the man. He told him that that fellow Cotton, whom people were talking about, had wanted him to join them (the conspirators), but he would not. He was going to Texas to get out of harm's way. The man rambled on telling about the designs of the conspirators. The man knew too much!

At the next town the gentleman had Saunders arrested on suspicion. He was brought back to Livingston. And on the strength of his testimony Cotton was immediately arrested again. Before the committee Saunders confessed that he had been asked by Cotton to join in the conspiracy, but he refused. He testified under oath that Cotton kept a bunch of Spanish horses turned loose in the woods which he used, as a pretext for hunting that he might have opportunity to talk with the negroes.

Cotton denied it all. He said that Saunders was prejudiced against him. It seemed that the committee was getting nowhere.

But suddenly the trial took a different turn. A planter from near Beatie's Bluff came leading one of his negro boys before the committee. The negro had acknowledged that he knew something about the contemplated insurrection. He was ready to testify. He said that one day, while hunting horses in a prairie, a white man, also hunting horses, had approached him and began to ask questions about the master: if he was a good man, whether the negroes were whipped much, and how would he like to be free? The negro told how the man had made him take a drink of brandy with him, and made him drink first. The man had told him he would inform him later when the insurrection was to take place. The negro did not know the man's name but believed he would recognize him if he saw him.

He was carried into a room where a dozen or more men were standing. Was the man there? The negro shook his head. No, the man was not there.

He was led to another room where Cotton was stationed with some half-dozen other men. He immediately pointed out Cotton, and boldly exclaimed: "That is the man who talked to me in the prairie."

Cotton "looked thunderstruck and came near fainting." He said nothing. He just sat there with a strained, blank stare on his face. The guards came and led him from the room that the committee might deliberate on his case.

Immediately after leaving the room he exclaimed to the guards, "It's all over with me! All I wish is that the committee will have me decently buried, and not let me hang long after I am dead."

"Great God," exclaimed a by-stander, "Cotton, you do not know that you will be convicted."

He replied despondently that the testimony was so strong against him that they must convict him — they could not avoid it.

It was suggested to him that it would be some atonement for his guilt to tell them who his accomplices were.

Later in the day he sent word to the committee saying that if they would pledge themselves not to have him hanged immediately, he would come out and tell them all he knew about the conspiracy.

The committee sent word that they would not pledge themselves to extend any favor to him. He might make a confession, however, if he wished.

Cotton asked for paper and ink, and without coercion wrote out a confession of his guilt in detail:

"I acknowledge my guilt, and I was one of the principal men in bringing about the conspiracy. I am one of the Murrell clan, a member of what we call the grand council. I counciled with them twice, once near Columbus, this spring, and another time on an island in the Mississippi River. Our object in undertaking to excite the negroes to rebellion, was not for the purpose of liberating them but for plunder. I was trying to carry into effect the plan of Murrell as laid down in Stewart's pamphlet. . . . Blake's boy, Peter, had his duty assigned him, which was, to let such negroes into the secret as he could trust, generally the most daring. Some negroes on most all the large plantations knew of it; and, from the exposure of our plans in said pamphlet, we expected the citizen would be on their guard at the time mentioned, being the twenty-fifth of December next; and we determined to take them by surprise, and try it on the night of the fourth of July.

"All the names I now recollect who are deeply concerned, are Andrew Boyd, Albe Dean, William Saunders, two Rawsons of Hinds County, who have a list of all the men belonging to the Murrell clan in this state, being about one hundred and fifty. . . . John and William Earl, near Vicksburg, in Warren County, Ruel Blake, of Madison County. I have heard Blake say he would make his negroes help, and he was equal in command with me. Lunsford Barnes, of this county; James Leach, near Woodville, Wilkinson County; Thomas Anderson, below Clinton, in Hinds County, and John Ivy, in Vernon. There are arms and ammunition deposited in Hinds County near Raymond."

He signed his name "Joshua Cotton," and handed the document over to the committee. A few minutes later the committee condemned him to be hanged. Within the hour he was led out under heavy guard to a tree. His execution had been rushed in the hope that the news of it would strike terror among others of the clan.

Under the gallows he acknowledged his guilt, and the justness of his sentence, and remarked, "it was nothing more than I deserved." And likewise he invoked "the vengeance of his God if every word written was not true;" and said further that all those he had implicated were as actively engaged in the conspiracy as he was.

As they were placing the rope around his neck someone asked if he thought there would be any danger that night.

The executioners gave him a few more minutes. He

turned toward the group and spoke slowly. "Yes," he
said, "if the others should not hear that I have been hung."

His last words were, "Take care of yourselves to-night
and to-morrow night."

William Saunders was tried on the 3rd. But it was
not until after Cotton had made his confessions and signed
them that the committee passed sentence upon Saunders.

Saunders had come into the country the fall before
and secured a job as overseer for a planter living near
Livingston. He had not remained at the job. His deportment was such as to induce his employer to discharge him.
He then became intimately acquainted with Cotton and
joined him in the practice "as steam doctor."

It came out during the process of the trial that he had
been a convict in the Tennessee Penitentiary for stealing,
and he had been ordered to leave his boarding place in
Hinds County because of his suspicious character. He
often stayed out all night without being able to give any
satisfactory reason. He was asked by the committee why
he had not revealed what he knew about the conspiracy as
soon as he had learned of it. He made them no satisfactory
answer.

But he had told the guards who brought him back to
Livingston that "Were I to disclose all I know respecting
the conspiracy, I would be shot down in ten minutes after
entering Livingston."

Most of the evidence that had applied to Cotton applied also to Saunders. The committee had before them the
evidence of the negroes who had been hanged at Beatie's
Bluff on the second. He was condemned by the committee
to be hanged; and late in the afternoon he was led out and
strung up alongside of Cotton.

The gruesome work of the committee had its effect.
Reports of the hangings spread from county to county.
There was no massacres. Apparently the quick drastic
action of the citizens broke the back of the conspiracy.
But the grim committee went on digging further and further into the workings of the plot. They sat in session at
Livingston from nine in the morning until four in the evening, according to the provisions of their by-laws. It was
a terrible, straining work. But they kept at it, investigating reports, trying suspects. Some who were accused convinced the committee of their innocence and were released.
Others were tried and given the death penalty, from which
there was no appeal; and day after day men were led from
the sultry trial room with ropes around their necks.

On the 6th Albe Dean was brought before the committee and tried. He had been arrested on the 3rd. He
was a "lazy, insolent man." Two years before he had
moved in from Ashford, Connecticut. He made a show
of earning a living by constructing washing machines, until he became acquainted with Cotton. He then abandoned
his business and turned steam doctor, associated with the
firm of "Cotton, Saunders & Company." He possessed a
habit very annoying to the Mississippi planters. He would
often come to the owners of runaways and intercede with
their masters to save them from a whipping. He also had
a habit of riding about the country "looking for horses."
On the way to Livingston he had asked about several negroes, and inquired if any of them had mentioned his name.
He was shocked to learn that they had implicated him, and
had already been hanged.

Perhaps the most convicting evidence against him was
that of Joshua Cotton. He had testified: "Dean was one
of my accomplices, and deeply engaged in the conspiracy,
as a member of the Murrell clan." He was sentenced to be

hanged. He died in dogged silence, neither acknowledging his guilt nor asserting his innocence.

He made one last request — that his name be kept a secret. He said his father was a public man, and it would break his mother's heart to hear of her son's ill fate.

On the morning of the 7th A. L. Donovan, a pale, nervous young man, was brought before the committee. A few hours later they sentenced him to hang.

Donovan had moved in from the North. His behavior had aroused the suspicion of the planters. Donovan, it was found, was a radical Abolitionist. When he found out that the clan was planning the liberation of the negroes, he immediately fell in with them. Whether or not he knew at first that they were a band of cut-throats and robbers who were not really interested in freeing the negroes but wished to use them as instruments to assist them in plunder, was not determined from the evidence. It seemed almost impossible, however, that he could have failed to learn of its real purpose. According to reports of the negroes he knew of the worst of it.

It was said that Murrell led many Abolitionists into the slave country to assist in the rebellion. "By Murrell's orders they made themselves gin-wrights, located in the cotton country and became blantly pro-slavery. Some of them bought slaves with clan money, instructed them in clan purposes, and set them to work among their fellows." Murrell always kept on hand an English lecture on slavery, which was one of the most convincing arguments of its day for the liberation of the slaves. He read it often and used its arguments. His clansmen used it also. Near the beginning of the lecture was the statement: "Could the blacks effect a general concert of action against their tyrants, and let loose the arm of destruction among them and their property so that the judgment of God might be visibly seen and felt, it would reach the flinty heart of the tyrant." Such sentiment applied to many Abolitionists. It is said that Murrell had personally fired Donovan with these Abolitionist ideas, and sent him into the slave country.

Donovan had been asked to leave the country, but had refused, alleging as a reason that he had to take care of some old keel-boats which were half sunk in Big Black River. He had been caught in close conversation with the girls who divulged the plot. It was found during the examination of the negroes at Beatie's Bluff that they would not talk in his presence. When he was told that he could not be present at the examination "he evinced considerable uneasiness, and kept walking to and fro."

Once Donovan was out of sight, a number of negroes implicated him, saying that he was "one of their leaders, and deeply implicated with them in the conspiracy." One of the negroes from Beatie's Bluff stated that Donovan had often solicited him to join them and had said "nothing was easier than for them to get their freedom, that the negroes could kill all the white people; and if they should be pushed, that he would take them to a free state."

A planter from Beatie's Bluff appeared before the committee and told of a strange conversation he had had with Donovan. The witness was at the time of the conversation working a gang of negroes in a field. Donovan had approached him and remarked that he would hate to be an overseer. The overseer, somewhat surprised, asked why. "There is too much whipping to be done," Donovan had replied. The man explained that he whipped the slaves only when they deserved it, and that was not often. "Well, my friend, you won't need that whip much longer." Donovan warned. "These negroes will be free," he continued, and he told how "they could obtain their liberty by force,

THE SOUTH WAKES UP

and that they would do it, not by themselves, but with the aid of thousands of rich, smart white men, who were ready to head them, with money, arms, and ammunition for their own use."

He had tried to force his way to talk to the negroes, "to inform them of their rights." He had received "a little good advice" and was threatened with the whip. He had left the field in a rage.

If it had not been for the fact that the Abolitionists were spreading propaganda of all sorts and trying to work upon the feeling of the negroes, Donovan's actions would doubtless have been taken much more seriously. He was considered at the time just another "crazed Abolitionist," and perhaps at the time under the influence of Stewart's book.

At high noon of the 8th he was led out, raving and blurting out his hatred for the slaveholders. Fighting and cursing, he invoked all the curses known upon the hated aristocrats, until the rope choked him into silence.

A few weeks later, a letter came to his address. It was turned over to the committee. It was from his wife in Maysville, Kentucky. It was a pitiful, touching letter full of anticipation of an anxious woman:

"My dear Angus (she wrote) . . . You say you have little hopes of receiving an answer to this (letter of his). Do you think that woman's heart is so hard, or that she could forget the one she once loved? No, she could not. Your conduct has grieved me more than you have any idea of, or I think you would not have done so. I feel thankful to hear that you have come to a full determination to break off from all your bad habits, and to study yourself and try to become a useful member of society; this I have long prayed for; I hope now my prayer is answered in some degree. O, my dear Angus, pray to God that He may change your heart, and give you grace to put those good resolutions in practice. I cannot consent to come there and live until I am fully convinced that you will not return to your former ways. . . . In the meantime I shall expect you to lay up something to commence housekeeping with . . . It is a great consolation for me to think of seeing you again, and once more enjoying your company. . . . I want you to write often; and I subscribe myself yours, affectionately, Mary."

But "Angus" was already rotting in a shallow potter's grave, where he had been cut down and thrown without ceremony.

A posse set out for Hinds County to find Lee Smith. They, found him in his own yard cleaning his guns. He saw them coming and made a start for a loaded gun. A shout from the men and pointed rifles set him back in his chair. They told him if he made a move he would be shot down in his tracks. He was "so alarmed as to faint." He asked if he had been charged by Cotton as being connected with the conspiracy (his arrest being made before he could have been appraised of Cotton's confessions).

Back in Livingston the committee went to work on his case. There was evidence before them to prove that he had been very intimate with Cotton and Saunders, and that he had worked with them in the steam practice. But there was a "multiplicity of evidence introduced to establish his good character." There was little evidence against him except that Cotton had named him. The committee decided that they would not punish him, the evidence being what it was. They requested, however that he leave the state at once. He left the committee room a relieved man. But he had no sooner crossed into Hinds County than he was taken by citizens of that county. He was lynched.

William Benson, a day-labourer, who was working for Ruel Blake, was brought before the committee. He was known to have made rash remarks, at one time telling the negroes that they ought to be free, and "with sticks alone they might whip the whites." There was damning evidence against him. But he was considered a great fool, "little above an idiot." They did not consider him responsible for his acts, so they ordered him to leave the country, and turned him loose.

Lunsford Barnes had been named by Cotton as being an accomplice in the conspiracy. He was reputed to be a "good, honest, hard working boy." Nevertheless he had been very intimate with Cotton, and it came out during the process of the trial that he had agreed to go to Texas with Cotton and sell stolen negroes for him. However the committee turned him loose after ordering him to leave the country. He was very ignorant and uneducated; and his youth had been considered.

John Ivy and Andrew Boyd escaped to the swamps of Big Black River. They were traced by bloodhounds all one afternoon; and again next morning a pack of dogs was close on their heels. Ivy found a horse beyond the swamps and made his escape. A few hours later the posse caught Boyd in a boggy canebrake. He was hanged.

The case of Ruel Blake was the strangest of them all. It was difficult for people to believe that he could be guilty. He was a planter and slaveholder, and he was a gin-wright of reputation. There was a peculiar dignity about the man. He had been a seafaring man in his youth, and he told of strange experiences upon the high seas. Some gathered from his wild stories that he had been a pirate. It was also the general impression that the man was addicted to boasting.

During the very first days of the excitement Blake's negro boy, Peter, had been brought before the committee. He was deeply implicated. He was an impudent, stubborn young negro who bluntly refused to talk, and said they could kill him first. And so his shirt was torn off his back and he was stretched over the big table in the committee room that served as a whipping block, for a few licks to "loosen up his tongue."

It was the custom for the slave holders to whip their own slaves, and so the whip was handed to Blake. He took the whip and swung it down on the boy's bare back. Over and over again he swung, with great motion; but the committeemen saw that he was not hurting the boy. He was only faking.

It was only natural that a good master hated to see his slaves whipped, and so no one suspected Blake. He was just too soft-hearted for the job, they concluded. They politely asked him for the whip. The lash was handed to a Mr. Johnson with the instruction to make the boy talk.

Now, the long black-snake began to dance stinging blows upon Peter's bare black back. He flinched and rolled his eyes, and then began an agonizing mumble. And then Blake came rushing through the crowd pushing men aside. "Stop," he stormed. "Any man that touches that boy another lick will have to whip me first." Johnson drew back for another blow. But he never finished it. Blake caught the whip stock, and the men were tussling over the whip. He was slinging Johnson around, when Johnson caught the loose end of the whip and popped at Blake's face with it. Blake floored him with his fist. Johnson had possession of the whip, and he came up crashing it into Blake's body. Blake was in the act of plunging into him when by-standers rushed in and separated the men. They dragged Blake out of the room. "Run," a friend cried out at him, "Johnson will kill you if he sees you again."

Blake rushed away down the street, his face streaming with blood, from a long gash made by his own whip. Citizens looked on in amazement. A neighbor, Captain Thomas Hudnold, saw him and was moved to pity. He insisted that Blake take one of his own horses and "get away until the excitement should subside." Then he had better come back and apologize.

Blake thanked him, and promised that he would. He dashed out of town in a fog of dust.

This was a strange proceeding. The citizens did not know how to take it. They could see no reason why a man of Blake's position should act so rashly.

Later in the day they resumed whipping Peter. But they stopped whipping him for fear that he might die from the blows. Peter was the one negro who never talked.

A few days later citizens realized that Blake would never come back. In the meantime it was proven that he was one of the chief instigators of the conspiracy. A five hundred dollar reward was immediately offered for him, dead or alive.

Over a week later he was found in Vicksburg. He had gone back to his youthful calling. He was posing as a Mississippi boatman.

They brought him back, with his hands tied behind. He was a doomed man already. There was doubtless more evidence against him than any other man that had been hanged. During the trial he just sat there in a rickety chair between his guards, silent and rigid. He looked like a man whose nerves had cracked. He said he was innocent, but he made no other defence.

His trial was the climax of the excitement. For days it had been thought that he would never be captured, and people had raved against him. Now the whole town turned out to see him hanged.

He protested his innocence to the last. Under the gallows he made some remarks about the committee, saying that they could not have done otherwise from the evidence before them. He tried to say something else but he only mumbled and stammered and could not be understood. His nerves had gone to pieces.

For days the committee room had been a busy scene of blood and passion. Terrifying confessions had been wrung from whites as well as blacks. Men had been startled and then scared half out of their wits by the revelations. Suspects had been dealt with severely, the citizens hardly knowing the immensity of the thing with which they dealt.

After the trial of Blake, the committeemen relaxed. Blake was the last of the Madison County conspirators to be tried. A few more minor cases were brought before them, and then they adjourned for a few days.

During the adjournment a posse from Warren County came over bringing the two brothers, William and John Earle, to be tried by the committee. They had previously been picked up as suspicious characters. But they had been released from the examining court after "proving" an alibi. Later it was found that they had sworn lies. Again they were arrested, and this time brought to Livingston. They were placed in jail until the committee could meet.

It took little urging to get a full confession from William. He was a vain, egotistic, headstrong fellow who took a curious pride in the fact that he had been one of the ringleaders in organizing the contemplated conspiracy, that he was to have been a captain, and that he had counciled with the "big bugs" of the clan. He saw that it was all over now. But he boasted that it would have been a different story if they had just had their chief.

The confession as copied by an attendant and signed by William Earle explained the whole plan of campaign. He listed the captains and named the territory that each was to attack ". . . . We expected to have force to visit the large plantations in the river counties, and, by the time we arrived at Natchez, we would take any place. We held out the idea to the negroes that they should be free; but we intended that they should work for us. . . . Spies were to go ahead on all occasions."

It was late in the night when he finished his confessions and signed them with a bold hand. They told him he would be hanged early in the morning. Then they left him.

But they never hanged William Earle. He cheated the hangmen of the job. For next morning when they came for him they found him swinging from the top rung of a ladder propped against the wall of his cell. He had hanged himself using a handkerchief for a rope. He was already cold and stiff.

When they told his brother of his ending, he rejoiced and said that he was glad William had hanged himself, that he would never have been in this trouble if it had not been for him. John said that if both had been released, he thought William would certainly have killed him for something he had divulged.

John Earle was arraigned before the committee and confessed his guilt. "I heard of the 'Domestic Lodge' in March last from Lofton, who showed me the sign of the lodge and wanted me to join it," he said. "They (the clansmen) were to have arms and ammunition at the Old Agency in Hinds County, in Yazoo Swamp, near Vernon, and at Baton Rouge." He said that he could not have told the secret because he had been told to "keep my mouth shut."

The committee found him guilty, and he was turned over to the citizens from Warren County.

One wonders what the convict chief in the Nashville penitentiary thought when he heard of the spasmodic ending of his monumental scheme. Doubtless he was disgusted.

CHAPTER XVIII

A NEW DAY

THE monster that Murrell had created and nurtured and then left an orphan had showed its vicious teeth and growled, but like some big, overgrown, clumsy reptile, its awkward movements and fumbles had brought its detection, and before it could either withdraw or strike it had been crushed. But its very appearance had thrown fear and alarm into the minds of the people.

The very madness of the Murrell plot had caused it to be discredited. Now it seemed that almost anything might happen! For months and years a bitterness had been growing between the two classes of society. But the changing frontier had always furnished activities to occupy the pioneer's mind. Hideous crimes had been committed; society had trembled and shuddered and then forgotten them in the changing events of the fickle frontier. Now the people in their anger began a widespread movement against the underworld. The dissipated culmination of the Murrell plot started a round-up of criminals along the entire river.

Vicksburg took the lead. Here the greatest, and longest remembered demonstration took place, though not entirely as a result of the plot exposure.

It was to a great extent local circumstances that started the Vicksburg purge. But once the citizens rose up they were determined to erase, as nearly as possible, this element from their city. They must take no chances on letting another organized plot get under way! Even before the trials at Livingston were completed, one of the Vicksburg outlaws set off the spark that started the local class war.

It all began while the citizens of Vicksburg were holding their Fourth of July barbecue. They were suddenly disturbed from their festivities by a noted gambler named Cabler. He had swallowed a few drinks of cheap whiskey in one cf the taverns under the hill; it had made him feel too good for his filthy surroundings. And so he came staggering up the hill, blowing, his eyes red. He pushed his way into the crowd of ladies and gentlemen. He swore he was as good as any of them. He was going to have a seat at the table, and "he'd be damned" if anybody stopped him. To avoid any distasteful demonstrations in the presence of the ladies a few thoughtful gentlemen proceeded to gently lead him away. He tore loose and plunged back toward the tables, raving, swearing, jeering at the aristocrats whom he hated. When he was approached again, he immediately knocked down one of the citizens with his fist.

Men rushed on to the gambler. The crowd went panicky. Women went screaming and scurrying about in all directions. Cabler would probably have been torn to pieces on the spot if officers had not taken immediate charge of him. They took him away and told him to keep traveling.

Later in the afternoon the town witnessed another confusion on the river side of town. It was announced that Cabler was coming back up, armed and determined to kill the officer who had led in putting him away from the feast. He swore he would kill the first one who bothered him. But before Cabler could make good any of his threats, two officers rushed forward and arrested him. They found on his person a loaded pistol and a large knife and dagger. The citizens were at a loss to know what to do with him. His crime had only been contemplated. Therefore the law could do nothing with him. And, on the other hand it would never do to free him; it would only increase his vengeance.

They determined to lynch him, there being no way to get him by law. But before the citizens could carry out the execution they softened. They decided upon a less severe sentence. Cabler was carried out under a guard, attended by a crown of citizens, tied to a tree, punished with stripes, tarred and feathered, and ordered to leave the city in forty-eight hours.

The news of Cabler's arrest blazed over the "district." A few confederates had tried to raise a force to rescue him. They had too little time to save him from his punishment. They determined on something bigger. Now they decided to rally and "take the town." The red light district became a swarming, raving mass, boasting and threatening. A few of the gambler's friends gained the courage to come up the hill. They did a good deal of loud talking and boasting among themselves for the benefit of bystanders. But it was all empty gesturing. Soon they were back in their dens along the landing, telling "what they would do yet."

The Cabler incident could not be forgotten. More definite reports of the conspiracy were coming in from the North. It was time something was being done! A general mass meeting was called at the courthouse.

Speeches were made about "shameless vices and daring outrages" of "professional gamblers destitute of all sense of moral obligation," who "support a large number of tiffin-houses to which they decay the youthful and unsuspecting," of street scenes of drunken and obscene mirth, disturbances of the public order and insults to citizens.

These brazen characters had thrived in spite of the law. No legal way had been found to handle them. But now the citizens were determined that this pack of "sporting gentlemen" should go. They drew up the following resolutions:

"*Resolved,* that a notice be given to all professional gamblers, that the citizens of Vicksburg are *resolved* to exclude them from this place and its vicinity; and that twenty-four hours notice be given them to leave the place.

"*Resolved,* that all persons permitting faro-dealing in their houses, be also notified that they will be prosecuted therefor.

"*Resolved,* that one hundred copies of the foregoing resolutions be printed and stuck up at the corners of the streets—and that this publication be deemed notice."

The next day was Sunday; but at an early hour the notices had been printed and each square of the city carried one. During the day a majority of the gang, terrified by the threats of the townsmen, dispersed in different directions, without making any opposition. It was hoped that the remainder would follow their example. The citizens on the hill waited for twenty-four hours. Then the military corps, followed by a file of several hundred citizens descended upon the "district." Gambling houses were visited and raided; faro-tables and other gambling apparatus were piled up in the streets and fire set to them. The "sporting gentlemen" and "ladies of pleasure" made a stubborn retreat, cursing and threatening as they went.

The gamblers retreated to a tavern owned by one of the gang named North. They barricaded, and promptly sent out the word that they "wouldn't move another damn step."

The house was surrounded and charged. Doctor Hugh S. Bodley, one of the leading physicians of the city, led the raid. But he never reached the house. A charge of buckshot at close range sent him slumping to the ground in a puddle of blood. Bullets were flying from all doors and windows.

When the citizens saw that Doctor Bodley was dead they rushed on the building with one mighty charge, firing as they went. They almost tore the house to pieces. The gamblers were dragged out like hogs from pens, wounded and bleeding and grunting. How many would have died from their wounds no one could say. The enraged citizens never gave them time to expire in this way. As soon as ropes could be secured they were hanged in the doorways along the street. And here they hung for the next twenty-four hours. It was so ordered "as a warning to all such characters."

Then the ropes were cut and they came flopping to the ground. They were tumbled into a cart, hauled away and dumped into a ditch and covered.

Accounts of the quick round-up at Natchez and the grim proceedings at Livingston spread rapidly over the

Valley and gave courage to lovers of law and order.
Peace officers were added to city forces, vigilant committees and patrols were organized to do away with lawless-
ness, clean-ups were begun in earnest. Other towns followed the example.

Memphis had its round-up.

The Gut was issued warning. The inhabitants sneered,
and threatened back. They would not be routed out like
rats! The place was soon working like a swarm of mad
bees. The inhabitants of the Gut let the town on the hill
know they were making bad medicine.

They took the initiative. They came sallying up the
hill. They swore they would burn the courthouse. They
were laughed at. They raved, and mouthed more oaths.
They would do worse; they would set fire to the entire
town. But they did not. They fired a few shots into
empty air, but they could never muster the courage to do
any real destruction. Later that night they dragged themselves back, exhausted by their own rage.

Then the citizens began their round-up in earnest.

Natchez-under-the-Hill also had its purging; and all
up and down the river from Cincinnati to New Orleans
the outlaws felt the reaction. Outlawry had reached its
climax.

For years the outlaws had preyed upon society along
the Mississippi River and the traces; and the law had
struck back only feebly. It had been left to Murrell to
give the outlaws an organized purpose as well as an organized hatred.

But his outlaw empire came crashing down. Once
the bandit chief was imprisoned, the days of the empire
were numbered. Without leadership, the terrible plot ex-

posed, the vengeance and determination of society upon them, the marauders had to change their course or travel. The old days had passed. . . . And it was Murrell's own scheming that had brought the end.

Chapter XIX

LAST DAYS

MURRELL continued to read his "old law book" in the
Nashville penitentiary. By the early part of 1837
he had devised an appeal. He employed two lawyers for
mouthpieces, told them that his case could be appealed, and
gave them instructions as to how to work. His petition
was granted.

In April of that year Sheriff J. S. Lyon of Madison
County went up to Nashville and brought Murrell back to
Jackson where he had been tried amid so much excitement
nearly three years before. Murrell had regained much of
his composure. (After a few months of raving and des-
pondency in prison, he had calmed down to study.) He
had bought a fine suit for the occasion. He held his head
up. He said that justice would be rendered yet.

But Murrell found a different scene at Jackson this
time. There was no excitement. Whether or not there
had been a flaw in the procedure of his earlier trial, or
whether he was guilty of stealing the Reverend Henning's
negroes were points of insignificance to the populace. It
had taken extreme dangers and risks for the people to be-

lieve the Murrell plot. Now that it had been exposed in such a frightening manner, they were not inclined to listen to technical arguments.

But the defendant still had confidence in his cunning intellect. His two lawyers, William Yerger and J. W. Chalmers made flowery appeals and spent hours on details. There was but little material to make a case. None of the clansmen dared risk their hides in order to testify for their chief. They had seen and heard too much of what took place at Livingston and the river towns. Enraged citizens had not cooled down yet. They would still have liked to get hands on anyone known to have had a part in planning their destruction.

The defense sent out a summons for Stewart. Perhaps they could break down his evidence this time. There was one chance in a hundred. But Murrell was desperate. He would try anything.

But Stewart could not be found. Shortly after the trial he had passed out of sight. No one could give the court any definite idea about where he might be located. The search only brought out confusing tales about the man: He had sailed for Europe, he was living in an obscure part of the country under an assumed name, he had been killed by clansmen when he attempted to settle in Texas.

The defense tried to make a point of everything. They said that Stewart was ashamed to show his face, that he knew his evidence would not stand up again.

Doubtless no outlaw except Murrell would ever have struggled against such futile odds. However, he fought until the last gap was closed—to the sad and bitter end.

But no one was impressed. Soon he was back at Nashville laboring with the other convicts inside the crowded wall of the state penitentiary.

On April 3, 1844, approximately four months before his ten years were up, John A. Murrell was pardoned.

And from that date on his history is fragmatory and legendary.

When Murrell emerged from prison this time he found a changed world. That is sure. His friends were gone, his clan was destroyed, the heyday of the outlaws had passed, law and order had gained the upper hand in the Valley.

His family had made a mysterious exit. But not before Elizabeth, too, had made a name for herself. About the time that John A. was convicted his sister was arraigned before the court in Jackson, convicted of larceny and sentenced for one year. But she was recommended for mercy, and at the last minute received a nominal fine. It seems that all the children took after their mother! It has been recorded that "the family moved out of the country." And that vague statement closed the record.

The final outcome of John A. Murrell's wife is also obscure. It had been said that she was one of the chief conspirators, that in her home in Madison County she entertained clansmen and heard the hellish plans of the negro rebellion discussed, and that through her the gang chief sent out instructions to his men while confined in Jackson. When he broke jail she was accused of smuggling saws to him. But it was never proven, nor were any of the other accusations against her. Whatever the relation or understanding between them was this woman hovered her man until he was definitely taken from her. Whether she was guilty of any crime or not, feeling was too high against the very name for her to remain in Madison County. Shortly after the trial she moved quietly out of the country.

One general account of the woman's life stated that "She shortly (after the marriage) found out the character

of the man, but nevertheless, remained a true wife until
his death." One wonders if she waited for him and they
were again united after ten years of separation, and spent
their last days together. Seemingly, no one can say.

A group of Tennessee historians have stated that after
his incarceration Murrell was broken in health and spirit,
and retired to the quiet little mountain village of Pikesville
in Bleadsoe County to spend his final days in peace and
quiet, reading his Bible, chatting with his friends, and
earning his living as a blacksmith, living to all appearances an upright life. His agreeable manner won him
friends there, to some of whom he freely admitted his
thievery, but always denied that he was guilty of murder.
He died of tuberculosis a few years later, so the version
goes.

There were a few interesting minor details of the story
that have reached print: "On his death-bed he wanted to
make a confession, but he was gagged and prevented by
friends, one of whom exclaimed 'Great God, John, don't
give us all away!' " Another writer said that "In preparing his body for burial the brand on his thumb was observed; also marks on his back left by the lash. His grave
was dug in a north and south direction to preserve its
identity. . . . He was buried in the Billingley graveyard,
a few miles north of Pikesville." But the grave of John
A. Murrell cannot be found in the Billingley graveyard nor
in any of the burying places around Pikesville.

But the historians, not to be outdone, explained this
simply enough. The body was dug up. But why the
disinterment? ". . . . It (the grave) was opened at night,
presumably by students of phrenology or medicine, and
the skull removed to be made a museum exhibit." A recent magazine writer gave his version: "This (his inter-

ment) should have ended his career. But it didn't. During his lifetime . . . Murrell had posed before many congregations as a living example of what it means to be righteous, and, remembering this, certain citizens of the South determined that in his death he be exhibited to the world as an example of what it meant to be wicked. They therefore repaired to the Billingley plot, disinterred Doctor Murrell, who of course took no interest in the proceedings, and hung him to a tree by the roadside."*

Now tradition has it that after Murrell came out of prison he returned to the old Neutral Ground country, and again became a bandit chief. And it is probable that he did. How much of a leader he was yet is something to guess at.

Murrell's talent lay in organization and management. And it is said that his old confederates rallied about him, and soon he had a gang around him that was the terror of the country. It is very probable that some of Murrell's early depredations in the Neutral Ground have been contributed to his later days.

If the legend is true, Murrell found a different situation in the Neutral Ground to what he had known before. In some respects it was possibly a better location for a freebooter: Traffic had increased across the territory, stage coaches carrying wealthy travelers were running regularly over the San Antonio and Nolan traces, immigrants on their way to the new Texas country were pouring through with all their belongings, great droves of horses and cattle were being herded from the plains of Texas and driven to the markets at Natchitoches and Alexandria, and back came the drivers with the rich proceeds. Pickings were still plentiful for the shrewd bandit.

---

* White, "On the Southern Circuit" (Collier's Oct. 4, 1930).

But these rich prizes had their off-sets. The year after Murrell emerged from the penitentiary, Texas became a state of the commonwealth, and the frontier along the Sabine River passed away. Troops had been massed at Fort Jesup until it was the strongest military post west of the Mississippi River, and these troops served as valuable police protection against the bandits. By the time the troops were called away to fight the Mexican War, the country had been settled by many law-abiding citizens. Certainly the outlaws did not enjoy the free hand that had been possible during the days of the Free State of Sabine.

It was too late for Murrell to stage a great comeback in the Neutral Ground territory. It is said that some of Murrell's men realized the situation before their leader, or perhaps they were not so bold as he. A certain John Cole went to the freebooter and suggested that they had better break up; too many people were flocking in from other states and settling. Cole insisted that the gang should scatter and go to Mexico if they still wanted to speculate. A few of the gang followed Cole's suggestion and went to Mexico. Murrell favored no such suggestion, and he considered all men who did cowards. He considered this break in his ranks as mutiny. And Murrell had a way of dealing with such matters.

The story came from a tottering old homesteader whose eighty years in the immediate vicinity enriched him with much local history and tradition. There was only one uncertainty in the story. He did not know exactly when it happened, but he had heard his father tell of it many times. Perhaps it makes no great difference; it gives some light on how Murrell maintained discipline among his men: A member of his gang by the name of Al Fox was sent to "talk to Cole." He was to notify the deserter that he either had to come back to the gang or he could not stay in the country. Fox found the man at his home sick in bed. The sick man told Fox that he would not talk, but he grumbled about coming back to the gang, it was too risky a business. The men seemed to be getting nowhere. And then Cole, somewhat numb from lying in bed so long, stretched himself. His gun was overhead on a rack, as was the arrangement in frontier homes. It was an innocent move, but fatal. Fox took the gesture, so he said, as an effort to reach his firearm. Fox drew his own gun and fired. Cole slumped over in his bed dead.

Certainly Murrell did not stay long in the Neutral Ground after he was released from the Tennessee State penitentiary. It may be that after a short stay in west Louisiana, he abandoned it and returned to the peace and quiet of his native Cumberlands, and therefore both versions of his last days are correct, in part.

One legend has it that Murrell was killed on Shird's branch at the foot of Hunt's hill in the Kisatchie community on the eastern border of the Neutral Ground and was buried on the bank of Kisatchie Creek. The details of the legend have made it appear logical. Murrell had what was known as little banks and big banks, and he had sent word to members of the gang that he wanted to move all the money to the big bank (possibly the cave). It was the general belief among members of the gang that their chief wanted to get all the money collected and then kill them. But instead, members of the gang plotted and killed him.

Another legend relates that he was killed near the Sabine River while making arrangements for some stolen horses.

Apparently, no one knows what became of Murrell.

CHAPTER XX

HIDDEN TREASURES

PERHAPS no outlaw in the South, with the probable exception of the pirate, Jean Lafitte, has inspired so much digging as has Doctor John A. Murrell. There seems to be no end of it. From the Devil's Punch Bowl on the Mississippi westward to the Sabine River continuous searching has been going on these many years.

The stories of Murrell's hidden treasures are legion. Some of them seem logical enough. Others appear as romantic exaggerations of dreaming minds, as queer and unintelligible as the life history of the land pirate himself. But they all form a part of that mysterious story that is Murrell's. And it seems that they will live on forever. Somehow, this life story would seem incomplete without them.

On the northern outskirts of Natchez on the Mississippi is a strange geographical phenomenon known as the Devil's Punch Bowl. It is a gigantic semi-circular depression in a bluff near the Mississippi River said to have been caused by a huge meteorite that fell on the bluff in prehistoric times. The pit covers several acres and resembles the crater of a long extinct volcano. This hole is credited with having been the rendezvous of various bands of pirates in days past, including the outlaw king, John A. Murrell. But what is remembered most is the fact that it was used as a banking place for ill-gotten treasures.

Strange accounts of scientific phenomenon have brought anxious seekers from afar with picks and shovels. For instance, captains of ships passing by this point report that their compasses are greatly disturbed; sometimes they spin completely around. Some authorities say that this is because of an immense amount of iron that was sunk into the earth by the falling meteorite. Others, remembering the old tales of outlaw days, say that the instruments' antics are due to the presence in the crater of great pots containing gold and silver coins.

Legend has it that the great pirate, Sir Henry Morgan, first visited the place and stored a loot there nearly a hundred and fifty years before the time of Murrell, and writers have pointed out the place as one of Lafitte's banks. Many other outlaws in time made this haven their residence and secreting place. That one band of outlaws might have found the loots of their predecessors and carried them away seems not to appeal to the logic of the treasure seeker.

It is not likely that Murrell spent much time at the Bowl. That place was a retreat for river pirates who preyed upon the river traffic. After Morgan, there were never any great loots on the stream to be taken as was the case on the Gulf in the heyday of the Spanish conquests. Immigrants and traders from up-stream formed the bulk of the traffic. The real prizes came up the Natchez Trace through the wilderness. Farmers from the upper country floated their produce down the river with the current, and with the market money started home overland. Murrell knew his trade. He waited until these river cargoes were turned into cash ready for spending. Along the trace prosperous gentlemen often traveled alone; and here was a convenient place to dispose of evidence. The whole set-up suited Murrell's system. Murrell was definitely a land pirate.

It is quite probable that Murrell had money hidden away with which to finance his rebellion. But there are reasons equally as logical to indicate that he never stored away great amounts. In the first place, his uprising was to be sudden, with followers striking simultaneously in different sections. It was to last but a short time. Secondly, prominent men were members of the clan, and they did their banking in the regular fashion. Much money from dead men's pockets found its way into regular so-called honorable bank accounts. And also, Murrell never took such great loots as did the pirates of the Gulf who preyed upon the Spanish treasure ships. Along the Mississippi, and certainly during his first religious campaign, he took his money as he needed it, usually from the lone travelers, or by petty swindling. And finally, Murrell was a spendthrift who turned his money loose as easily as he gained it. If the clan as an organization had put away large sums of money for their ventures, there is no reason why they should not have had ample opportunity to repossess them.

In the Neutral Ground the situation was somewhat different. Over the San Antonio and Nolan traces came the riches of the West. It was easy picking until the United States government established Fort Jesup almost in the heart of the old Free State of Sabine. Many mule loads of silver from the Mexican mines were lost here to bandits. But Murrell did not get in on the choicest of these prizes. He took his fórtune mainly from traders on the way home from market or from the eastern prospectors on their way to buy property in the West. From caravans, lone travelers, and cattlemen from Texas, Murrell robbed with an audacity that was characteristically his own.   There was little for which to spend money in this frontier country; and in as much as the loots were often comparatively large, and the gang was often forced to make hurried getaways, it is most probable that Murrell hid money in the Free State of Sabine.   And there are many people in Louisiana who believe that they have written proof of the fact.

More than one person in the Neutral Ground vicinity has spent a lifetime digging, surveying, collecting maps and other data that would uncover the treasures that Murrell left.   There is a great amount of secrecy about these things.   In the Neutral Ground country one might live for years without knowing that one's next door neighbor was a treasure seeker.

One of the largest collections of treasure-finding materials, so far as the writer knows, was that owned by an acquaintance, who lived all of his life in the vicinity of the old Neutral Ground.   He was for many years a public figure, a man prominent in the affairs of his state.   It was only after his death that the writer knew of his extensive interest in hidden treasures.   The collection, though larger than the average, is typical.

It was through the courtesy of a son that the privilege of seeing this collection was extended, though only after being respectfully informed that no photographs or notes were to be taken.   Some of the data was withheld. But the collection viewed filled an unusually large trunk. There were scores of maps and charts of more varieties than one would guess existed.   Hours were spent, in company with the son of the deceased collector, studying the instruments in this curious "treasure" trunk.

To attempt to piece a complete story from these mysterious documents would be like fitting a jig-saw puzzle which has many important cuttings missing. They are fragments, and in the main, vague fragments at that. It is a complicated picture puzzle because many characters enter into it. How much history these instruments tell is a matter of conjecture.

The charts and way-bills of this trunk deal with, in the main, three characters, Murrell, Captain Smith and McKay (sometimes spelled McCay). The exact relations between these men and Murrell is not entirely clear. History would make us believe that Murrell died before the others and that his colleagues moved westward with the frontier. There are two theories about Smith. Some say he was a brilliant steamboat captain on the Mississippi. Another version has it that he had been an army captain. Doubtless it did not matter on the frontier; his title seems never to have been questioned.

A traditional account of Smith describes him as six feet tall, dark haired, and handsome. McKay is described as short and stout, with sandy hair and moustaches.

These bills, strange as it may appear, are not only clothed in mysterious language, but in most brilliant phraseology. There is a vague baffling consistency about them all. The bills would indicate that the author, or authors, was most familiar with astronomy, theology, poetry, history, and Freemasonry, for such is the language in which these instruments are written. The clues rest upon missing words, deceiving words, etc. The charts have missing links; part of the keys to these have been found, but there seems to be something missing about most of them. One key, for instance, was from a book of theology entitled *The Advent of the Twelve Apostles*.

Many of the phrases used are philosophical, such as:

"The grave is the end of all earthly pain," "A bird of a feather will flock together," "Search and ye shall find," "The evil of the world shall be judged," "The just shall receive their reward." Much reference is made to the mercy and goodness of Jesus Christ, the plan of salvation, the day of reckoning, the reward of goodness and the punishment of evil. Many references are made directly to the Deity in the most brilliant and elevated language. Strange talk, indeed, for bandits! But Murrell would have delighted in such inconsistencies.

The solar system is mentioned with surprising accuracy. Egyptian hieroglyphics are alluded to, and apparently some attempt made to use them. The language of Freemasonry proved conclusively that the writer or writers, of some of the instruments was learned in Freemasonry of the higher degrees. Numerous references are made to the Royal Arch Chapter. A supposed clue to one treasure, for instance, was given in terms of a lodge hall. One enthusiastic seeker was able upon unraveling the clue, to line-up and establish on the side of a hill the perfect lay-out of a masonic lodge room. It was not a difficult task. For buried charcoal was found just as the chart indicated, and other described instruments of a masonic nature buried as markers were uncovered. It was the supposition that the treasure in question would be found at the position of the treasurer's desk in the lodge hall. Incidentally the search was futile. Doubtless the whole thing had been framed, or else someone had approached the treasurer's desk already.

All sorts of designs and figures are represented on these bills—stars, arrows, cubes, circles, hearts, squares, octagons and many other geometrical drawings of curious fashion. Among the several animals used are the cow, horse, mule, lion, bear.

Some of the figures are as amusing as they are meaningless. One chart of interest pictured two wrenches,
with these remarks written at either end: "Some nuts are
smaller than the wrench. Others are larger." It advised
further that "All things that appear foolish are not foolish
—some things that are wise appear foolish, some that appear foolish are wise."

Many of the charts refer to "the four banks." And
this is the vital part in which every treasure-seeker is interested. They are given the following approximate location: Murrell's Cave, in the Kisatchie community (already described), Mull Beth, likely near Grande Ecore,
and probably at times referred to as Grand Ecore; Black
Lake Bank, in the vicinity of the lake by that name in
Natchitoches Parish; Mesquite Tree, nine miles west of
Natchitoches on the old San Antonio Trace, "to the west
of the road on a hill at the head of a branch which runs
into Spanish lake following a northward direction."

The story goes, in connection with this mesquite tree,
that Murrell brought the sprig from Texas to use as a
marker for buried treasures. It is a conspicuous fact that
mesquite trees do not grow naturally in this country.
Mention is made of the fact that mesquite trees grow
slowly, and that in the space of fifty years there would
be only three or four trees that would come from the orig-
inal. It is stated that the "mesquite" treasure was a cara-
van of bullion captured on a route from Vera Cruz. The
soil has been well cultivated around this lonesome mesquite
tree by treasure seekers.

One unusual parchment gives a description of the four
banks in pure poetry. But it is all meaningless; the pretty
rhymes only mystify. For it is expressively told that
words and phrases are misleading, and one thing may mean
another. The names of states often mean rivers, and

boundaries and towns and streams, states and other things. The bandit poet had a talent for confusion.

The charts are written on various kinds of materials —paper, parchment, leather, cloth, rocks; one map was crudely carved on a piece of board; and there were a few pieces of peculiarly stained glass and crock which seemed to have no meaning, but apparently had a value for the treasure seeker. These documents are of almost every size and form. One of the larger measured about six by eight feet. Some of the impressions were made with ink, others with pencil, crayon, stain, and some were carved.

There was one letter among the documents that seemed clear enough, at least there were no missing words, and it offered some explanation about a number of the "treasure bills." The letter is supposedly that of an old negro by the name of Taylor. The letter explains how he was intrusted as a messenger in carrying a number of these charts, and at one time had a practically complete set. But he got into trouble—the exact nature of the difficulty is not clear—and in his confusion his instruments were lost, or rather scattered. He reveals the story of many years spent in running down and recovering these papers. With a little help—financially, mainly—he believes that he may yet recover the missing ones. In spite of the fact that the whole thing gives the impression of trickery, considerable faith has been attached to this letter. It supposedly authenticates a number of pieces of the collection.

How many mysteries this old trunk contains is a matter of speculation. These would seem to be enough documents to find any treasure, if there are any. But this great collection is by no means exhaustive. There are other collections, said to be just as extensive. And there are minor sets. The extent of this fantastic research cannot be estimated.

There seems to be no end to digging in the vicinity of Murrell's Cave in the Kisatchie community. The cavern long ago caved in, closing all entrances, and apparently forever sealing its secrets. But treasure seekers will not despair at finding or making another.

A few years ago the writer visited an old settler who had spent over eighty years in this community. It was said of him that he knew much of the doings of Murrell. He was a very weak old man with a trembling voice, who would shake at the thrill of his own stories. He was in bed at the time, too feeble to be up.

He related a few wild tales that he had heard of Murrell from people older than himself. But he kept drifting back to the subject of Murrell's treasures. And a sparkle would come to his sunken eyes at the thought of them: "There's no telling," he said, "how much money is buried around that old cave!" And for some strange reason he was sure it had not been taken away. Later he became confidential: "That treasure is going to be found soon," he emphasized.

He explained that he had a son in New Orleans who had gained the "inside dope." He was at the time negotiating for financial assistance. "He's got the map we have been looking for for years. . . . I only hope I live to see what Murrell left in that cave."

The old gentleman was left with his hope of dying rich. He had exhausted himself with his own enthusiasm.

Little was thought of the old man's story until a visit was made to the scene of the cave a few weeks later. The ground had literally been blown to pieces with high explosives.   But the soil had been blasted away only to uncover the solid rocks below.   A few rocks had been moved near the entrance, but beneath them there were still more impassable obstructions.   No entrance had been made.

Even if the long sought map was correct, it was of no avail.   But the old gentleman did not share in the disappointment.   A few days after the visit he passed away— happy perhaps in the thought that his family might yet share the treasures that Murrell left.   Treasure seekers apparently never lose courage.   The stimulating hope of recovering buried fortunes becomes a sort of disease with them.

This old settler's story is not so important within itself; it is a typical story of the old-time treasure hunter. With all their errors and vain hopes there is something strangely dramatic about them.   Such characters lend a romantic flavor to this mysterious country of buried secrets.

So through these many years the trails of the preaching bandit-king have been followed with pick and shovel. Perhaps so long as the story of Murrell lives men will listen and then set to digging.

BIBLIOGRAPHY
BOOKS

Baldwin, Joseph G., *The Flush Times of Alabama and Mississippi.* San Francisco, 1883.

Belisle, John G., *History of Sabine Parish, Louisiana.* Many, Louisiana, 1912.

Coates, Robert M., *The Outlaw Years.* New York, 1930.

Davis, James D., *History of the City of Memphis.* Memphis, 1873.

Dunbar, Seymour, *A History of Travel in America*, Indianapolis, 1905.

Foster, Austin P., and Moore, John Trotwood, *Tennessee the Volunteer State.* Chicago, 1923.

Fulkerson, H. S., *Early Days in Mississippi.* Vicksburg, 1885.

Gould, E. W., *Fifty Years on the Mississippi.* St. Louis, 1889.

Guild, Josephus Conn, *Old Times in Tennessee.* Nashville, 1878.

Hale and Merritt, *A History of Tennessee and Tennesseans.*

Howard, H. R., *The History of Virgil Stewart.* New York.

Keating, J. M., *History of the City of Memphis and Shelby County, Tennessee.* Syracuse, N. Y., 1888.

Life and Adventures of John A. Murrell. T. B. Peterson and Bros., Philadelphia, publishers.

Moore, John Trotwood, and Foster, Austin P., *Tennessee the Volunteer State.* Chicago, 1923.

Old Times in West Tennessee. By "a descendant of one of the first settlers." Memphis, 1873.

Phelan, James, *A History of Tennessee.* New York, 1888.

Phillips, Ulrich B., *Plantation and Frontier Documents, 1649 - 1863,* vol VII. Cleveland, 1909.

Raine, William M., *Famous Sheriffs and Western Outlaws.* New York, 1929.

Saxon, Lyle, *Fabulous New Orleans.* New York, 1928.

Walton, Augustus Q., *A History of the Detection, Conviction, Life and Designs of John A. Murrell, the Great Western Land Pirate.*

Williams, J. S., *Old Times in West Tennessee.* Memphis, 1873.

Williams, Samuel Cole, *Beginnings of West Tennessee, 1541 - 1841.* Johnson City, Tennessee, 1930.

Yoakum, B. F., *History of Texas.* 2 Vols. New York, 1856.

DOCUMENTS, PERIODICALS, ETC.

Anderson, Douglas, "A Famous Outlaw of the Early Southwest," *The Nashville Banner* (March 20, 1921).

Archivo General y Publico, Mexico City.

Case, Harold M., "The Devil's Punch Bowl and the Land Pirate John A. Murrell," *The Tensas Gazette* (St. Joseph, Louisiana, February 17, 1933, a reprint).

Cox, Isaac Joslin, "The Louisiana-Texas Frontier," *Texas State Historical Association Quarterly,* X and XVII.

Journal of the House of Representatives of the State of Tennessee for the years 1845 - 1846.

Marshall, Park, "John A. Murrell and Daniel Crenshaw," *Tennessee Historical Magazine,* VI.

McCullock - Williams, Martha, "John Murrell and His Clan," *Harpers* (Jan., 1897, vol. XCIV).

Phares, Ross, "The Neutral Ground of the Free State of Sabine," *The Shreveport Journal* (June, 1935) ; "The

Neutral Territory in Louisiana," *Louisiana Club-woman* (May, 1930); "Outlaws of the Neutral Ground," *The Shreveport Times* (April 14, 1935); "Philip Nolan and His Ghost Road," *The Shreveport Journal* (Aug. 26, 1935); "San Antonio Trace ... Oldest Road in the Southwest," *The Shreveport Times* (June 28, 1935).

"Piratical Mystery of the Devil's Punch Bowl," The *Commercial Appeal* (Memphis, May 28, 1933).

Scrapbooks of Mrs. Cammie Garrett Henry, Melrose, Louisiana.

Scrapbooks found in the Tennessee State Library, Nashville, Tennessee.

Sugar, Leon, "Following the Spanish Trail Across the Neutral Territory," *The Louisiana Historical Quarterly*, X.

Tait, John Leisk, "When Murrell was Merciful," *The Commercial Appeal* (Memphis, 1912).

White, Owen P., "On the Southern Circuit," *Collier's* (October 4, 1930).

OTHER AIDS

In addition to written sources the author is indebted to many old-timers in the Neutral Ground territory and along the Mississippi and the Traces for information concerning Murrell and the land in which he operated. To Mrs. Cammie Garrett Henry of Melrose Plantation especial thanks are due for the full use of her extensive library. Appreciation is here expressed to Mrs. Ora Garland Williams, Reference Librarian, Louisiana State Normal College, Natchitoches, and Mrs. Kathleen DeCou Thain, teacher of languages, Louisiana Polytechnic Institute, Ruston, both of whom read the entire manuscript and offered many helpful suggestions.

INDEX